CHINA'S POLITICAL AND ECONOMIC TRANSFORMATION: THEORY AND CASE STUDIES

CHINA IN THE 21ST CENTURY SERIES

China Naval Modernization:
Implications for U.S. Navy
Capabilities
Ronald O'Rourke
2008. ISBN: 978-1-60456-709-0

Is China A Threat to the U.S.
Economy?
*Craig K. Elwell, Marc Labonte
and Wayne M. Morrison*
2008. ISBN: 978-1-60456-843-1

Is China A Threat to the U.S.
Economy?
*Craig K. Elwell, Marc Labonte
and Wayne M. Morrison*
2008. ISBN: 978-1-61668-067-1
(Online Book)

Congress and US China Policy
Jian Yang (Editor)
2008. ISBN: 1-56072-844-2

Human Rights in China
Lee R. Massingdale (Editor)
2009. ISBN: 978-1-60741-116-1

China: Has the Last Opportunity
Passed By?!
Guang Wu
2009. ISBN: 978-1-60741-538-1

Business, Finance and Economics
of China
Lian Guo and Fai Zong (Editors)
2010. ISBN: 978-1-60741-299-1

China's Political and Economic
Transformation: Theory and Case
Studies
Rongxing Guo
2010. ISBN: 978-1-60876-321-4

CHINA IN THE 21ST CENTURY SERIES

CHINA'S POLITICAL AND ECONOMIC TRANSFORMATION: THEORY AND CASE STUDIES

RONGXING GUO

Nova Science Publishers, Inc.
New York

For permission to use material from this book please contact us:
Telephone 631-231-7269; Fax 631-231-8175
Web Site: http://www.novapublishers.com

NOTICE TO THE READER

LIBRARY OF CONGRESS CATALOGING-IN-PUBLICATION DATA

Guo, Rongxing.
  China's political and economic transformation : theory and case studies / Rongxing Guo.
     p. cm.
  Includes index.
  ISBN 978-1-60876-321-4 (softcover)
  1. China--Economic policy--1976-2000. 2. China--Economic policy--2000- 3. China--Politics and government--1976- I. Title.
  HC427.92.G855 2009
  330.951--dc22
                            2009041986

Published by Nova Science Publishers, Inc. ✛ *New York*

谨以此书
献给我的大姐二姐
荣莲(1950–)和荣爱(1955–)
她们在最困难时期的弃学务农
不仅为我们家庭提供了生活保障
也使我顺利完成了学业

*This book is dedicated to
my sisters, Ronglian and Rong'ai,
whose early participation in farming activities
(at the cost of discontinuing their schoolwork) not only
provided various necessities for the living of
our family members but also helped me
to complete my academic work
during those difficult
years*

CONTENTS

LIST OF FIGURES

LIST OF TABLES

PREFACE

There have been a large number of studies on China's political and economic transformation over the course of recent decades. However, it seems that most, if not all, of these studies have the following shortcomings. First, past studies lack effective theories by which to explain China's non-linear pattern of political and economic transformation. As a result, most of them are problem driven, not theory driven; they are motivated by a desire to account for particular events or outcomes. And they are devoted to the exploration of cases, not to the elaboration of theory. Secondly, few in-depth case studies at micro-levels have been found in existing studies.

In this book, I will provide not only theoretical explanations for but also macro- and micro-level case studies on China's political and economic transformation. When we refer theory, we refer to rational choice theory and, most often, to the theory of games. However, our advocacy could apply to other forms of theory as well as to simulation techniques (such as system dynamics) that could be used to the quantification, though at a rough extent, of these theories. Most of the case studies selected in this book are based on my previous field inspections to small politically-sensitive areas and the micro-level surveys on a few of former state-owned firms in China. Due to their unavailability to researchers both within and outside China, these case studies can provide a superb collection of materials for researchers and students with an interest in the study of the characteristics of Chinese transformation and for ordinary readers wishing to keep a closer watch on China's political and economic transformation.

Chapter 3 is based on the Global Research Project (GRP) entitled 'Understanding Reform' sponsored by the Global Development Network (GDN). I have substantially benefited from the collaboration with Professor Kaizhong Yang (BJDI/Peking University, China) and Professor Renwei Zhao (Institute of

Economics/CASS, China). Many valuable comments and suggestions on part of or the whole manuscript were received from the following individuals: Professor José María Fanelli (University of Buenos Aires, Argentina), Dr Gary McMahon (GDN and the World Bank), Ms Isher Ahluwalia (Indian Council for Research on International Economic Relations), Professor Richard Cooper (Harvard University), Professor Amara Pongsapich (Chulalongkorn University, Thailand), Professor Leong Liew (Griffin University, Australia), and several anonymous reviewers.

This book also includes some previously published materials. Specifically, Chapter 4 is based an article published in Chinese by the *Management World* (guanli shijie) with Li Shi and Xing Youqiang (2003, pp. No. 4, pp. 103–11). The major part of Chapter 5 is based on my monograph (*Cross-Border Resource Management*, Amsterdam and Boston: Elsevier, 2006, pp. 197–226). Thanks go to the co-authors of and the copyright owners of the above publications for their kind permission of my using these materials in this book.

Rongxing Guo
Beiqijia town, Beijing
2009-6-17

Chapter 1

INSTITUTIONAL DYNAMICS: AN ANALYTIC MODEL

1.1. A BRIEF NARRATIVE

From the foundation of the PRC in 1949, the Chinese government had uneasily followed the Soviet Union and adopted a centrally planned economy (CPE). Generally, this kind of planning system has the following problems. First of all, it makes almost all productive enterprises subordinate to administrative organs. To a large extent, this neglects the economic independence of the enterprises and thereby leads to the neglect of their material interests and responsibilities, blunting the levels of initiative and enthusiasm. Secondly, the system involves excessive command planning from above and is overly rigid. So long as the enterprises meet their stipulated targets, they are considered to have performed satisfactorily – regardless of whether or not its products satisfy the needs of society.

In the Third Plenum of the 11th Chinese Communist Party Central Committee (CCPCC), held on 18 December 1978, Deng Xiaoping and his senior supporters took decisive control of the CCPCC. This ended what has been described as two years of uncertainty and indecisive strategy and policy following the death of Mao Zedong. The Third Plenum of the Eleventh CCPCC, which was held in December 1978, marked a major turning point in China's reform and development. After a decade of turmoil brought about by the Cultural Revolution (1966–76), the new direction set at this meeting was toward economic development and away from class struggle. The course was laid for the Chinese Communist Party (CCP) to move the world's most populous nation toward the ambitious targets of the Four

Modernizations in sectors of industry, agriculture, science and technology and national defence.

In brief, the institutional evolution in the Chinese economy since 1978 has demonstrated a gradual process and may be outlined by the six phases listed below:

(1) centrally planned economy (before 1978);
(2) economy regulated mainly by planning and supplementally by market (1978–84);
(3) commodity economy with a plan (1985–87);
(4) combination of planned and market economy (1988–91);
(5) socialist market economy with *state* ownership as main form (1992–97);
(6) socialist market economy with *public* ownership as main form (from 1998 onwards).

Guided by the CCPCC (1984), the roles of central planning and market regulation were reversed in the modified system 'commodity economy with a plan'.[1] Generally, Phase 3 was known to be based loosely on the Hungarian model of market socialism. Nevertheless, the state continued to own the bulk of large and medium-sized enterprises and to regulate the production and pricing of a number of strategic commodities, but the market mechanism was permitted to play an increasing role in the pricing and allocation of goods and services and in the allocation and remuneration of labor in some non-strategic sectors. In the ideological struggles between the radical reformers and the conservatives, there was a new term 'socialist commodity economy'[2] from 1988 to 1989, but this was replaced by Phase 4 ('combination of planned and market economy') immediately after the Tian'anmen Square incidents of May–June 1989. Nevertheless, Phase 4 was extremely important insofar as it legitimated the abolition of traditional mechanisms of central planning system in favor of the introduction of market regulation.

During the 1980s, China's reform and open-door policy resulted in an increase in economic prosperity, but also led to some political and social instabilities. This can be witnessed by the CCP's 'anti-spiritual pollution' and 'anti-bourgeois liberalization' campaigns in 1983 and 1987, respectively. This

---

[1] Even though the term 'commodity' in the Chinese understanding is closely related to the concept of market economy, we may assume that it was used here to distinguish the Chinese economy literally from the Western-style market system.

[2] The term was firstly publicized in bold headlines in the CCP's official newspapers (such as *People's Daily* and *Workers' Daily*) in early 1988.

kind of political disequilibria between the CCP conservatives and intellectuals reached its high point in 1989, which, together with other factors such as high inflation and official corruption, eventually became a leading cause of students' protests against the CCP and central government during May–June 1989. As soon as the aftermath of the Tian'anmen incident had subsided, there was a shift of power in economic decision-making from reformers to conservatives. This led to a temporary brake being placed on China's economic reforms and also its rates of economic growth.

At the beginning of the 1990s the socialist camp in Eastern Europe and the former Soviet Union both suffered sudden collapses. China's immediate reaction to the collapse of these communist regimes was a policy of re-centralization, but the CCP soon realized that its legitimacy could be sustained only through economic growth brought about by further reforms. Amid the political deadlock between the reformers and conservatives concerning how to combine the planned and market economic systems, Deng Xiaoping made his now famous southern tour to the province of Guangdong in early 1992. Drawing on regional support for continued reforms, Deng's visit tipped the political balance at the CCPCC and the central government. This resulted in China's official declaration in October 1992 of its intention to build a 'socialist market economy,' as well as a calling for faster reforms and economic development.

In the early 1990s, some of the policies applied to the coastal special economic zones (SEZs) were extended to a list of inland regions and cities along the Yangtze river and, as a result of China's diplomatic normalization with the former USSR, to the border cities and towns adjacent to Russia and other neighboring countries. Furthermore, many inland cities, which did not qualify for these special treatments, established numerous economic and technological development zones (ETDZs) inside their regions. It is worth noting that the wide-ranging pro-development reforms during the above years brought about not only high economic growth but also the two-digital inflationary pressures that occurred in 1993. Facing with an overheating economy, the Chinese government announced a series of banking and financial reforms in 1994, which were aimed at eliminating some of the structural inefficiencies in the financial sector.

China's ambitious agenda geared towards transforming the Chinese economy into a market-oriented one was unveiled as early as 1992, when Deng Xiaoping's Southern Speech[3] eventually had an influence on China's decision-makers. On 14 November 1993, the formal document entitled 'Decision of the CCPCC on Several Issues Concerning the Establishment of a Socialist Market Economic

---

[3] For details of the Speech, see Deng (1992, pp. 370–83).

Structure' was finally approved by the Third Plenum of the 14th CCPCC. According to the decision, the government should withdraw from direct involvement in enterprise management. Instead, 'Government functions in economic management consist mainly of devising and implementing macroeconomic control policies, appropriate construction of infrastructure facilities and creation of a favorable environment for economic development' (Article 16). The Plenum also declared that 'the government shall take significant steps in the reform of taxation, financing, investment and planning systems, and establish a mechanism in which planning, banking and public finance are coordinate and mutually check each other while strengthening the overall coordination of economic operations' (Article 17).

The 15th National Congress of the CCP, held in 1997, saw a historic breakthrough in terms of the reform of the ownership structure of the national economy. The three aspects of the adjustment were: (a) to reduce the scope of the state sector and to withdraw state capital from industries that were considered nonessential to the national economy; (b) to seek various forms for materializing public ownership that can generally promote the growth of the productive forces and to develop diverse forms of public ownership; and (c) to encourage the development of nonpublic sectors of the economy such as the individual business sector and the private sector and to make them important components of a socialist market economy (Wu, 2005, p. 86). In September 2003, as the "Decision on Issues Regarding the Improvement of the Socialist Market Economic System" was adopted by the Third Plenary Session of the 16th CCPCC, it indicated that China's economic, social and political reforms will continue to be advanced comprehensively in the years to come.

China's commitment to the creation of a market-oriented economy has been the central plank of its program of economic reform, and considerable progress towards this end has been achieved since 1978, through the gradual withdrawal of the government from the allocation, pricing, and distribution of goods.[4] To date the reforms introduced have exhibited remarkable results. Particularly praiseworthy are the facts that the Chinese-type reforms have avoided the collapse in output characteristic of transitions in other former CPEs and generated unprecedented increases in the level of living standards across the country. Over the course of the past few decades, China has successfully implemented a stable economic reform and opening up to the outside world and, in particular, achieved a faster economic growth than any other socialist or former socialist countries in the world.

---

[4] See Appendix 1 at the end of the volume for a list of major reforms.

1.2. THE DYNAMIC MODEL

Past reform events show that in China the institutional improvement towards a market-oriented system followed a non-linear pattern. From the late 1970s to the early 1990s, China's reform indicated a recurring pattern of reform and retrenchment identified by a four-stage process: 'decentralization immediately followed by disorder, disorder immediately followed by concentralization, concentralization followed by rigidity, and rigidity followed by decentralization', a cycle of 'decentralization (*fang*)–disorder–concentralization (*shou*)–rigidity.' Since the institutional decentralization and concentralization might occur simultaneously in different sectors, authors with different analytical purposes may identify the *fang–shou* circle differently. For example, Baum (1994, pp. 5–9 and pp. 369–76) offers a plausible explanation of the *fang–shou* cycle during 1978–93: the decentralization (*fang*) policy was concentrated on 1978, 1980, 1982, 1984, 1986, 1988, and 1992; while the concentralization (*shou*) policy was concentrated on 1979, 1981, 1983, 1985, 1987, 1989, and 1993. In addition, Shirk (1993), Dittmer and Wu (1993, pp. 10–12) reach a similar conclusion, sketching out four relatively complete, synchronous cycles of *fang* and *shou* during 1980 to 1989: *fang* predominated in 1979–80, 1984 and 1988, while *shou* predominated in 1981, 1985–86, 1987, and 1988–89.

As a matter of fact, the *shou–fang* circle represents the dynamic process of the political games between radicals and conservatives. Specifically, the fang (decentralization) was initiated by the radicals, while the shou (concentralization) was insisted upon by the conservatives.[5] In this section, we will present an analytic model by which to examine the dynamic behaviors of China's market-oriented reform under different initial and exogenous (domestic and external) conditions. Frankly speaking, there is no single, well-defined political and institutional framework for carrying out market-oriented reforms. For example, in most cases, a market-oriented reform implies a reduction in the depth and scope of government participation and interference in an economic activity; in other cases, however, government intervention is necessary (see, for example, Williamson, 1995; Rodrik, 1996).

To avoid the ambiguity, we would temporarily put aside the Chinese economy. Instead, we consider a highly simplified CPE (centrally planned economy) which is transformed toward a market-oriented economic system within

---

[5] As a result of their very nature (as stated at Chapter 2), both radicals and conservatives have compromised with each other's initiatives during most, if not all, of the reform era.

a given time period. Specifically, the CPE is characterized by the following assumptions:

I.   A reform scheme may be either accelerated or reversed, depending on the improvement or deterioration of political stability, respectively.

II.   Political stability is associated with three factors – public satisfaction (as will be defined in Assumption III), social shock resulting from the reform, and external irritation (which is positively related to the extent to which the CPE opens its economy to the outside world).

III.   Population is treated as constant. Public satisfaction is positively related to the increment of income level.

IV.   External environment refers to economically marketized and politically democratized economies. The CPE's open-door policy has two effects: economically, it will promote economic growth through foreign trade and FDI inflows; politically, it will affect political stability through external irritation (as defined in Assumption II).

In order to simulate the CPE's reform process and its outcomes under different initial and exogenous conditions, we must identify the correlations between the important factors that can influence the dynamic behaviors of the CPE endogenously. Figure 1.1 shows a simplified model in which the feedback mechanisms are based on the assumptions made above. The exogenous (policy) variables and the initial conditions of the CPE are set as the following:

- The length of time for reform (T) is fixed at two values: $T=2$ (it denotes 'big bang reform'); $T=10$ (it denotes 'gradual reform').
- The initial stock of market-regulated economy (I_0) ranges from 0.0 (that is, there is zero share of market-regulated economy at the start point of reform) to 1.0 (that is, there is a 100% share of market-regulated economy at the start point of reform).
- The initial income (per capita and total) is set as $Y_0=\$100$.
- External policy (O) has two values: $O=1$ (it denotes 'open-door policy'); and $O=0$ (it denotes 'closed-door policy').[6]

---

[6] Here we use a much simpler definition of a closed economy than the others. Sachs and Warner (1995), for example, define a closed economy as one that has one of the following characteristics: non-tariff barriers cover 40 percent or more of trade; average tariff rates of 40 percent or more; a black-market exchange rate that is depreciated by 20 percent or more relative to the official rate, among others.

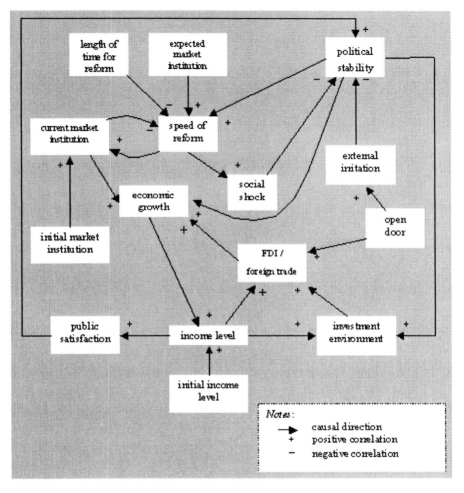

Figure 1.1. A simplified model of economic reform.

1.3. QUANTIFYING THE MODEL

In order to quantify the model built as above, we use system dynamics (SD) – a modeling method that first appeared in Forrester (1959). This SD, which was developed on the basis of conceptions in control theory, organization theory, and on the available techniques of computer simulation, can be used to simulate the dynamic behaviors of the CPE under different initial and exogenous conditions. It is a unique tool for dealing with questions about the way in which complex systems behave through time.[7] Before building a system dynamics model, one must identify the correlations between the important factors that could influence the dynamic behaviors of the system of our interest endogenously. According to the principles of system dynamics, social systems, no matter how complicated, are composed of different feedback loops. A positive feedback loop means that the target grows without any limit, while a negative feedback loop will not grow after the achievement of the target.[8]

In order to enable the quantitative model suitable for computer simulation, we use DYNAMO (an abbreviation of 'dynamic model') software developed by Richardson and Pugh III (1981). There are two categories for quantification of the causal relations described in our feedback model mentioned in Figure 1.1. The first category of causal relations includes those that can be precisely formulated. For example, the 'current market-regulated economy' (CGI) and 'speed of reform' (SOR) are formulated as the following:

$$CGI_k = CGI_j + DT \times SOR_{jk}, \text{ with } CGI_0 = I_0 \tag{1.1}$$

$$SOR_{kl} = \frac{EGI - CGI_k}{T} \times Q_k \tag{1.2}$$

where, j, k and l are time marks, and j<k<l. DT is represented by the time interval from j to k (or from k to l). I_0 and EGI denote the initial market-regulated economy and the expected market-regulated economy, respectively. In our analysis, EGI=1 (indicating that the policymakers expect a 100 percent of market-regulated economy after the reform is completed), and I_0 ranges from 0 to 0.5. The length of time of reform (T) represents how long the reform will last.[9] As defined in Assumption I, Q is used here to denote whether the reform goes ahead, stops, or is reversed. Specifically, it has three values: $Q=1$ denotes that the reform goes ahead (which needs that the value of political stability (PS) is larger than 1); $Q=0$ denotes that the reform stops (which needs that the value of PS is equal to 1); and $Q=-1$ denotes that the reform is reversed (which needs that the value of PS is less than 1).

The other category of causal relations includes those that can be determined only roughly. The rationale for this simplification relies on the fact that our analysis is not to precisely predict a set of time-series outputs of the

---

[7] One of the most influential research using the SD methodology would include Meadows (1972).
[8] For more knowledge about the SD approach, see Forrester (1969) and Day (1985, pp. 55-64).
[9] Obviously, $1/T$ represents the average speed of the reform.

macroeconomic indicators, but to show the general tendency of how the performances of the CPE will depend on exogenous variables. To this end, we use the following formula to determine the political stability (PS):

$$PS_k = PS_j + DT \times DPS_{jk} \tag{1.3}$$

$$DPS = 2.0 \times GR - 5.0 \times SOR - 0.03 \times O \tag{1.4}$$

In Equation 1.3, DPS denotes the change of PS; and in Equation 1.4, GR is growth rate, and O=1 (for open-door policy) or 0 (for closed-door policy). GR=EG/Y (EG, which will be defined in Equation 1.6, is economic growth, and Y is the size of national income[10]). In our analysis, we stipulate that, in order for the reform to go ahead (that is Q=1), the value of PS is assumed to be slightly larger than 1 (say, 1.001) at the starting time of reform.

There are also some dependent variables that can be more precisely formulated based on the existing literature. However, this will increase the complexity of calculations by involving more explanatory variables. We will therefore simplify their mathematical formulations. For example, with regard to the determination of the foreign trade and FDI, we create a comprehensive term – foreign economic contribution (FEC), though the latter is not exactly the sum of foreign trade and FDI. The FEC is simply determined by the following formula:

$$FEC = 0.05 \times Y \times O \times IE \tag{1.5}$$

where Y=income level; IE=investment environment (which is positively related to political stability and income level).

As defined in Assumption VI, economic growth (EG) is contributed by three sources – the current market-regulated economy, the domestic political stability, and the foreign trade and FDI (that is, FEC). We use the following equations to roughly formulate the CPE's economic growth (EG) and the income level (Y), respectively:

$$EG = \{0.1 \times CGI + 0.03 \times Min(Q, 0)\} \times Y + 0.5 \times FEC \tag{1.6}$$

$$Y_k = Y_j + DT \times EG_{jk} \tag{1.7}$$

---

[10] Since we have defined the size of the population as constant in Assumption III, the size of national income and income level are used interchangeably here.

where CGI denotes the level of current market-regulated economy, and, as mentioned earlier, Q has three values, 1, 0 and −1. Since CGI is 0.3 and Q is 1 at the time zero, the economic growth expressed in Equation 1.6 will be: EG=(0.03+0.03) ×Y+0.5×FEC at the beginning of reform. With regard to the determination of FEC in Equation 1.5, given that O=1 and IE=1, we have FEC=0.05×Y. We assume that the initial income level of the CPE is \$100, that is, Y_0=\$100 in Equation 1.7.

The level of investment environment (IE) and the change of investment environment (DIE) are determined by the following equations:

$$IE_k=IE_j+DT\times DIE_{jk} \tag{1.8}$$

$$DIE=1.0\times GR+0.5\times DPS \tag{1.9}$$

where GR=growth rate, DPS is defined in Equation 1.4. At time zero, the status quo of investment environment is assumed to be positively related to PS_0 and Y_0: that is, IE_0=1.0+$PS_0\times Y_0$/1000.

Compared with other methods (such as econometrics), system dynamics (SD) does not pay much attention to the accuracy of the values of specific parameters. In addition, due to the lack of any universal methods available, the test of the effectiveness of the SD model is much more difficult than that of the data based statistical and econometric models.

With regard to the sensitivity analysis of our SD model, we intend to clarify how the simulated results are sensitive to the parameter changes. In doing so, we try to calculate the degree to which the result of a simulation is sensitive to the changes of the parameters of the simulation. Numerically, the value of SSR_N (N=1 and 2) in Table 1.1 is the percentage change of the simulated result (SR_N) with respect to a one-percentage change of the parameter monitored. Obviously, the smaller is the value of SSR_N, the higher the effectiveness of the simulation (SR_N) is. From Table 1.1, we can find that, except for some simulated results for SR_1, the degrees of sensitivity are around or less than 1.0, indicating that the simulated results are not sensitive to parameter changes. More important is that the simulated results on $Y_{T=10}/Y_{T=2}$ are not sensitive with respect to the parameter changes. In addition, since the simulated results reported in Table 1.1 are those of the last stage of the period monitored, the average level of estimation errors would be reduced if the whole period is considered.

Table 1.1. Sensitivity analysis of the simulated results

I_0	Income level under gradual reform ($Y_{T=10}$)				
	SR_B	SR_1	SSR_1	SR_2	SSR_2
0.0	148	150	0.068	146	0.135
0.1	194	242	1.227	186	0.427
0.2	314	410	1.533	291	0.727
0.3	499	718	2.192	453	0.924
0.4	762	1194	2.837	680	1.073
0.5	1082	1766	3.158	1025	0.530
I_0	Income level under big bang reform ($Y_{T=2}$)				
	SR_B	SR_1	SSR_1	SR_2	SSR_2
0.0	182	200	0.507	179	0.143
0.1	216	256	0.918	209	0.337
0.2	297	378	1.372	274	0.762
0.3	401	563	2.020	380	0.524
0.4	579	986	3.516	538	0.707
0.5	865	1527	3.828	817	0.554
I_0	Ratio of income levels under gradual and big bang reforms ($Y_{T=10}/Y_{T=2}$)				
	SR_B	SR_1	SSR_1	SR_2	SSR_2
0.0	0.815	0.750	0.399	0.816	0.008
0.1	0.898	0.945	0.262	0.890	0.093
0.2	1.058	1.085	0.126	1.062	0.038
0.3	1.245	1.275	0.123	1.192	0.423
0.4	1.316	1.211	0.399	1.264	0.394
0.5	1.255	1.157	0.391	1.253	0.012

Notes: (1) All simulations are based on $Y_0=100$ and $O=1$ and the simulated results are only reported for the last output (i.e., Time=20). (2) SR_B denotes the basic simulated result (as reported in Figure 1.3); SR_1 denotes the simulated result in which the parameter of CGI (that is, 0.1) in Equation 1.6 is replaced with 0.12; and SR_2 denotes the simulated result in which the parameter of GR (that is, 2.0) in Equation 1.4 is replaced with 1.8. (3) SSR_1 and SSR_2 are the degrees to which the simulated results of SR_1 and SR_2 are sensitive to parameter changes, respectively. They are measured as follows:

$$SSR_N = \frac{\left| \dfrac{SR_B - SR_N}{SR_B} \right|}{\left| \dfrac{P_B - P_N}{P_B} \right|}$$

where $N=1$ or 2; P_B and P_N are the parameters assigned for the basic and new simulations respectively; SR_B and SR_N are the simulated results for the parameters P_B and P_N respectively; and SSR_N is the degree to which the simulated result of SR_N is sensitive to a change of the parameter from P_B to P_N.

1.4. THE SIMULATED RESULTS

To evaluate how institutional evolutions are influenced by reform strategies and initial conditions and external policies, we run the above model under different values of I_0, O and T (the standard DYNAMO equations are shown in Appendix 2). The simulated results (shown in Figure 1.2) may help us to derive the following corollaries.

> *Corollary 1.* Initial institutional conditions decide the extent to which a reform is successfully implemented. Specifically, the initial stock of market-regulated economy encourages the smooth implementation of the reform; while the initial stock of centrally planning institutions retards the smooth implementation of the reform.
>
> *Corollary 2.* External environment plays an important role in a market-oriented reform. Specifically, an open-door policy encourages implementation of a reform; while a closed-door policy retards the implementation.
>
> *Corollary 3.* Reform strategy matters in the whole reform process.

With regard to the case of the simplified CPE, we can investigate how the economic differences between the gradualism and the big bang are related to the initial market institutions. In Figure 1.3, the vertical axis is represented by ratio of the income level of the gradualism (T=10) to the big bang (T=2), that is, $Y_{T=10}/Y_{T=2}$.[11] Obviously, gradualism is better than big bang if $Y_{T=10}/Y_{T=2} > 1$, while big bang is better than gradualism otherwise. Since $Y_{T=10}/Y_{T=2}$ equals to 1 when I_0 is around 1/6 for open-door policy ($O=1$) and when I_0 is around 1/3 for closed-door policy ($O=0$) in Figure 1.3, we can derive a set of optimal strategies for reform under different initial and external conditions (see Table 1.2). Consequently, Corollary 3 includes the following:

> *Corollary 3.1.* When there is only a very small stock of market-regulated economy, big bang is better than gradualism.
>
> *Corollary 3.2.* When there is a large stock of market-regulated economy, gradualism is better than big bang.

---

[11] For simplification, we only use the income levels at the final stage of reform (that is, at time 20 in this simulation) in calculation.

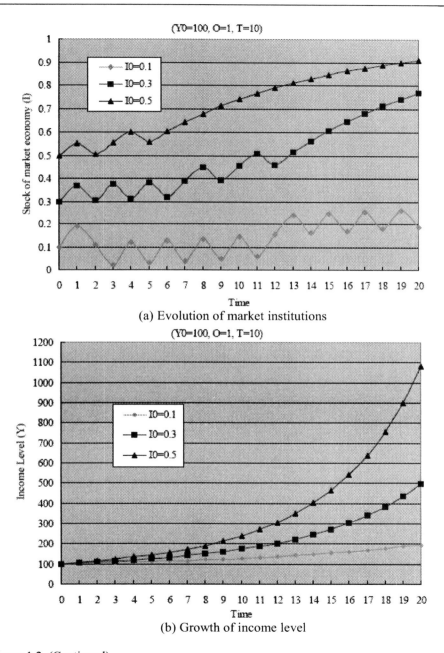

(a) Evolution of market institutions

(b) Growth of income level

Figure 1.2. (Continued).

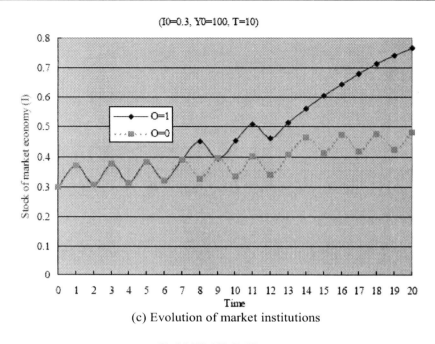

(c) Evolution of market institutions

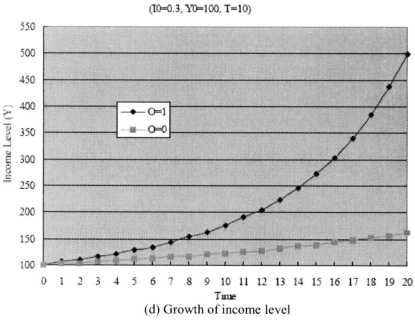

(d) Growth of income level

Figure 1.2. (Continued).

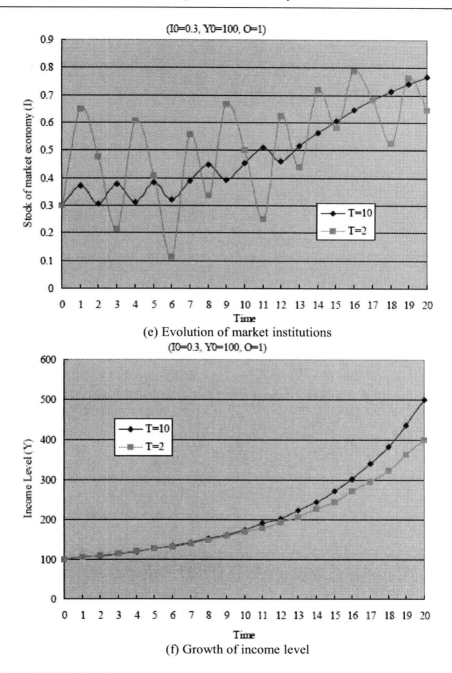

(e) Evolution of market institutions

(f) Growth of income level

Figure 1.2. (Continued).

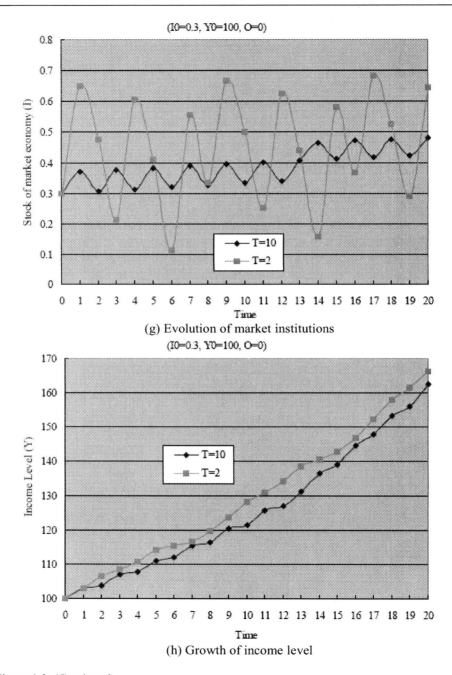

(g) Evolution of market institutions

(h) Growth of income level

Figure 1.2. (Continued).

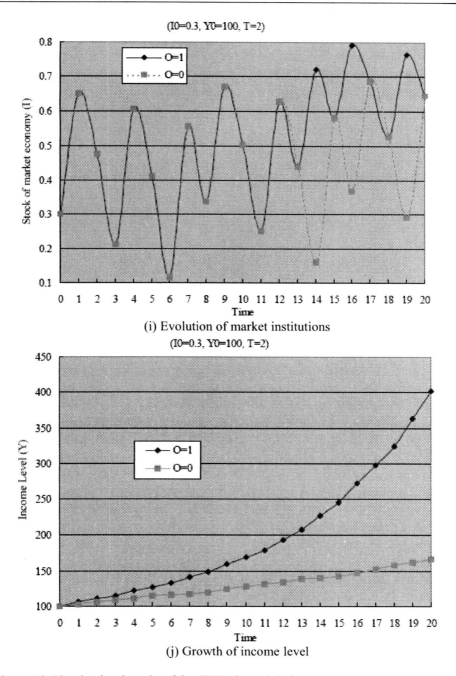

(i) Evolution of market institutions

(j) Growth of income level

Figure 1.2. The simulated results of the CPE's dynamic behaviours.

Corollary 3.3. When there is a moderate stock of market-regulated economy, external environment matters in the optimization of reform strategies. Specifically, gradualism is better than big bang under open-door policy, while big bang is better than gradualism under closed-door policy.

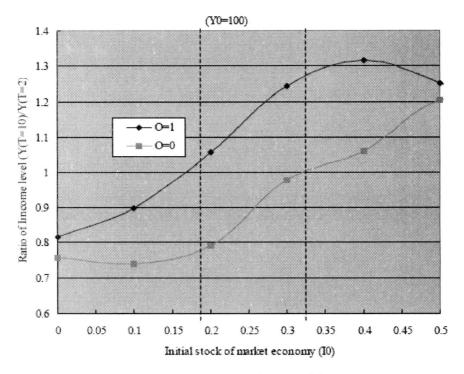

Figure 1.3. How reform strategy matters under different conditions.

It is reasonable to assume that the CPE has relatively weak market institutions at the beginning of the market-oriented reform, while at the late stage its market institutions will be improved as a result of the reform implemented during the early stage. Consequently, Corollary 3 can be roughly translated into the following:

Corollary 4.1. During the early stage of reform, big bang is better than gradualism.
Corollary 4.2. During the late stage of reform, gradualism is better than big bang.

Corollary 4.3. During the middle stage of reform, big bang is better than gradualism under closed-door policy, while gradualism is better than big bang under open-door policy.

Chapter 2

INTEREST GROUPS, STAKEHOLDERS AND REFORM

In this chapter, we allow reform to be determined endogenously. Our task is to find how the interest groups and stakeholders interact with each other throughout the whole process of the reform and how they have had a decisive influence upon the reform outcomes. For the simplicity of analysis, we assume that the CCP is the only player (policymaker), and that it can be further divided into different cliques (such as radicals and conservatives) in different reform periods. Interest groups can be defined as collections of individuals who share a specific common interest. It is noteworthy that the various interest groups can overlap. For instance, the same individual can be both an entrepreneur and a university professor. Stakeholders then are members of an interest group whose interests are affected by a particular decision.

The evidence described below will demonstrate how Chinese economic reform has evolved from the collusion of the CCP radicals and conservatives (during the early stages of reform) to the collusion of all political, economic and cultural elites (during the later stages of reform) as well as how this evolution has influenced the outcomes of the Chinese reform per se.

2.1. RADICALS AND CONSERVATIVES IN THE EARLY REFORMS

To understand the implications of the incentives for the implementation of a reform in China, we must make a point of the relationship between the CCP radicals and conservatives.[1] Both Deng Xiaoping and his senior supporters in power had been victims of the Cultural Revolution (1966–76) during which Mao criticized them for economic liberalism. The special events of Cultural Revolution meant that – regardless of their liberal or conservative ideology – they must unite or, at the very least, must not challenge each other in mutually tolerable matters during the early period of reform.

One of the initial challenges facing the Chinese leadership was to provide for the creation of a rational and efficient governing system to support economic development. In pursuit of that goal, the cult of personality surrounding Mao Zedong was unequivocally condemned and was replaced by a strong emphasis on collective leadership. An example of this new emphasis was the CCP's restoration in February 1980 of its Secretariat, which had been suspended since 1966. The new CCP constitution, adopted in 1982, abolished the post of CCPCC chairman – a powerful post held by Mao Zedong for more than four decades, thereby providing a degree of balance between the CCP radicals and conservatives.

The striking feature of the Chinese reform during the 1980s was the collusive game between the radicals and the conservatives. In considering a reform strategy, the radicals must take into account not only the benefit from the reform but also the political cost stemming from the possibility of losing their coalition with the conservatives. Since deterrence implies cost, the reform strategy that both players (radicals and conservatives) would find optimal to cooperate does not equate the marginal economic benefit with the marginal economic cost. Instead, a player's optimal strategy of reform equates the marginal economic cost with the marginal economic and political costs. In other words, it is political cost that creates a wedge between the efficient and optimal strategies of reform.

Although the strategy of pursuing faster reforms maximizes the radicals' gross payoff, it does not maximize its net payoff. The radicals would find it optimal to have a strategy involving slower reform in which the marginal economic gains from cooperation equal the marginal political and economic costs.[2] For example, Li Peng's long-lasting political career as premier is one of the outcomes resulting from the collusion of the radicals and conservatives. In 1987, Li became a member of the Politburo's powerful Standing Committee, and a year later Deng Xiaoping picked Li to succeed Zhao Ziyang as premier after

---

[1] In fact, it is difficult to consistently identify the radicals and conservatives throughout the whole period of reform. Those who had been treated as radicals during one period might become conservatives at a later stage; furthermore, a CCP senior who can be a radical reformer in respect of one agenda (such as agricultural or other domestic sector reform) might be considered as a conservative in another (such as external economic sectors or political reform in general).

[2] Note that this result does not depend on the process through which the redistribution of incomes from the radicals and conservatives has been determined.

Zhao had become the CCPCC's general secretary. This choice might have been seen as unusual because Li Peng did not appear to share Deng's advocacy of economic reform. However, it illustrated clearly that Deng had to seek compromises with the conservatives.[3]

Since the late 1990s, a new Chinese terminology – Baiping – has been popularized in mainland China. The term 'Baiping' is composed of two Chinese characters – 'bai' (to place, to put, to arrange, etc.) and 'ping' (flat, uniform, fair, etc.). The original meaning of Baiping is 'to put flat; or to arrange uniform.' The term had been so informal before the 21st century that even the 1999 edition of *Cihai* – the largest and the most influential Chinese dictionary published by Shanghai Cishu Publishing House – didn't collect it. Notice that the frequently used Baiping has extended from its original meaning to 'to treat fairly', 'to compromise', 'to tradeoff', 'to punish' and so on.

After the death of Deng Xiaoping in 1997, Jiang Zemin must deftly play its various wings against each other. In this scenario, Li Peng, Chairman of the eighth National People's Congress (NPC), was selected to hold the No. 2 post of the Chinese Communist Party Central Committee (CCPCC), higher than that of Zhu Rongji – Premier of the State Council – during the 1998–2003 tenure. This was the first in the PRC's history that NPC Chairman held a political rank higher than that of Premiership. Moreover, a large number of non-Communist party and non-party personages were selected as state leaders with the titles of vice Chairpersons of the NPC and of the Chinese People's Political Consultative Congress (CPPCC) in exchange of their support of the CCP as the permanent ruler of the state. For example, as for the 2003–2008 and the 2008–2013 tenures, China's state-level leaders have included nine standing members of the CCPCC Politburo (some of whom also held the posts of President, Premier, the NPC and CPPCC Chairmen) and dozens of vice Chairpersons of the NPC and of the CPPCC. The total number has been the highest since the 1980s.

As a matter of fact, during the massive mandatory retirement program which was facilitated by a one-time buyout strategy (this will be analyzed in Section 3.1 of Chapter 3), the outgoing CCP officials were partially compensated, in both economic and political terms. For example, a special name was coined for this kind of retirement, *lixiu* – literally 'to leave the post and rest'. After *lixiu*, retired officials continued to enjoy all of their former political privileges, such as reading government circulars of the same level of confidentiality. Some served as special counselors for their successors. As economic compensations, they could keep using their official cars with chauffeurs and security guards. In addition, officials

---

[3] Cited from http://edition.cnn.com/SPECIALS/1999/china.50/inside.china/profiles/li.peng/.

under *lixiu* received an extra month of wages each year and extra housing that their children and grandchildren were entitled to enjoy after their death (Li, 1998, p. 394). As will be discussed in section 3.1 of Chapter 3, without that reform, in which many younger cadres were able to play an important role, the reforms that followed afterwards would have been impossible.

In considering the profitability of more rapid reforms, the conservatives take into account not only the benefit from the reforms but also the political cost stemming from the possibility losing supremacy over the society. Since deterrence implies cost, the reform strategy that both players (radicals and conservatives) would find it optimal to cooperate does not equate the marginal economic benefit with the marginal economic cost. Instead, a player's optimal strategy of reforms equates the marginal economic cost with the marginal economic and political costs. In other words, it is political cost that creates a wedge between the efficient and optimal strategies of reforms. Although the efficient strategy of reforms maximizes the radicals' gross payoff, it does not maximize its net payoff. The radicals would find it optimal to conduct slower reforms in which the marginal economic gains from cooperation equal the marginal political and economic costs.[4]

When dealing with the early reforms, it is necessary to mention other stakeholders as well as their attitudes towards reforms. Farmers and urban workers — two groups that benefited from the reform-driven economic growth — did not oppose the CCP, and the reform in particular. Intellectuals, especially those who had received Westernized training and been seriously mistreated during the Cultural Revolution, adopted a more critical stance. They had a strong desire for Western democracy. On the other hand, however, the CCP elites, especially the CCP conservatives, could not at all accept a totally Western-oriented reform (Kang, 2002). Since the radical reformers had been much less powerful than the CCP conservatives at the period when most CCP seniors were still alive, their attempt at uniting with intellectual elite failed the during Tian'anmen incident in June 1989.

It seems likely that, as a result of the disappearance of the CCP seniors and the conservatives on the one hand and the emergence of more young and Western-learning officials on the other, the Chinese reform should have become increasingly radical since the mid-1990s. What does the evidence tell us?

---

[4] Note that this result does not depend on the process through which the redistribution of incomes from the radicals and conservatives has been determined.

2.2. POLITICAL, ECONOMIC AND CULTURAL ELITES IN THE LATER REFORMS

As the initiation and sustainability of a reform requires political, economic and cultural support, the identification of interest groups and stakeholders of the reform in general, but especially those who are politically (and otherwise) active as allies and opponents of reform, is an important step towards the successful completion of the reform. An important distinction is whether interest groups and stakeholders are organized – in other words, whether they pursue their common interest jointly in a coordinated fashion. It is natural to believe that stakeholders will exert pressure on policymakers. This, however, need not always be the case, as not all stakeholders are organized (Fidrmuc and Noury, 2003). Because organized interest groups are better informed than the citizenry at large, they can provide key personalities (the government officials, legislators) with intelligence of various kinds.

Beginning in the mid-1980s, the bureaucratic reform generated a large surplus of government officials. At the same time, many government agencies began establishing business entities, and bureaucrats became managers of these businesses. As a result, a phenomenon that later came to be known as *xiahai* ('jumping into the ocean'). Since the early 1990s, *xiahai* has been an immensely popular phenomenon among Chinese government officials.[5] By joining the business world, the former bureaucrats obtain much higher economic payoffs as well as personal freedom, despite being exposed to increased economic uncertainty. On the other hand, there is a high demand for those bureaucrats, since in the half-reformed economy many non-state enterprises need their knowledge and skills in order to deal with the remaining government regulations.

Since the 16th National Congress of the CCP, held in Beijing in November 2002, CCP membership has been formally opened to China's business elite. The removal of the clause in the CCP's constitution that officially prohibited private businessmen from becoming party members and serving in the government is intended to bring the CCP constitution into line with the reality of the party's character and social composition as it prepares to accelerate the pace of market reforms. In a rambling opening address to the Congress, Jiang Zemin articulated

---

[5] In a survey conducted in 1992, 30 percent of surveyed officials were thinking about *xiahai* (Chen, 1993). In another survey of local government officials in 1995, close to 20 percent were planning on *xiahai* (SCSR, 1996). Of those, 35 percent were looking for joint-venture enterprises, 21 percent for private enterprises, and 1.5 percent for SOEs. Tang and Parish (1998) find in their large survey that 99 percent of those officials who planned to quit the bureaucracy wanted to join businesses. – Cited from Li (1998).

the class interests of the new Chinese elite. He called for the Beijing regime to persevere in opening up to the capitalist market and declared that the CCP should protect the 'legitimate rights and interests' of businessmen and property owners (Jiang, 2002). The formal opening of the CCP to business layers in 2002 represented a turning point. The fact that Jiang's 'Three Represents' theory formalizes what has already emerged was highlighted by the year 2002 *Forbes* magazine list of China's 100 richest multi-millionaires. One-quarter of those on the list declared that they were CCP members (Chan, 2002). In addition, many Chinese CEOs of private companies or transnational corporations also have connections with the CCP.

Since the mid-1990s, cultural elites (including noted intellectuals, popular entertainers and ethnic minority-based social elites) have been getting close to political and economic elites in China.[6]

The factors resulting in the collusion of the political and cultural elites might include the following.

First, the disappearance of senior CCPCC members has weakened the power of the conservatives since the early 1990s, while the younger political leaders are usually more highly educated than their predecessors.

Secondly, after the Tian'anmen incident, radical intellectuals were subjected to serious retaliation, most of them either fleeing the country or disappearing from academic circles.

Thirdly, the changing external environment (such as the collapse of the former Soviet Union followed by the unsuccessful big-bang reform of Russia and the U.S. transferring from standing against the CCP to against China) helped most, if not all intellectuals to cooperate with the CCP and the government.

Several books have portrayed the post-Tian'anmen period as one of intense political disagreement (see, for example, Fewsmith, 1999; and Lam, 1999). Certainly, this was true until the mid-1990s. Yet disagreements since this time have been expressed increasingly through non-sanctioned means by non-sanctioned actors.

The elite battles evident today are based upon illegitimate end-running, not legitimate contestation. Thus the politics of contestation – legitimate competition within the structures of the polity properly used by a range of agreed actors – remains absent.

---

[6] This can be witnessed by, for example, Yu's (2004) article in which some influential Chinese economists are criticized for their favoritism to the rich vis-à-vis the poor.

The earnestness of contestation in the early reform era has been replaced by the anomie of compliance or the intrigue of crypto-politics in the post-reform era (Gilley, 2004, p. 121).

Among China's rural peasantry and the industrial working class, a seething hostility is building up over official corruption, poverty, the loss of services, unemployment and the widening income gap between rich and poor. After several years of factional debate within the CCP, a consensus has emerged that the lesson to be drawn from the Tian'anmen events is that the regime must build a solid base among the urban upper and middle classes, while making no democratic concessions to the masses (Chan, 2002). The government believed it could weather the opposition of workers and peasants by keeping them like 'scattered sand', lacking any national organization or coherent political program (Kang, 2002). Commenting on the sentiment of the political establishment, Kang (2002) points out: 'There is a stable alliance between the political, economic and intellectual elite of China. The main consequence is that the elite won't challenge the CCP and the government. The economic elite love money, not democracy. Their vanity will also be satisfied as the CCP has promised them party membership and government positions.'

How has the Chinese reform been linked to the collusion of the political, economic and cultural elites?

First of all, faced by the example of the failure of the radical reforms in the former USSR, the political elite – no matter how radical they had been during the previous period of reform – has become increasingly pragmatic over time. In essence, they would now be more likely to choose a more gradual/partial (or alternatively, less radical) reform strategy than they had chosen in the 1980s.

Secondly, the political, economic and cultural elites have increasingly become beneficiaries of the existing system that was based upon the past gradual and partial reforms.

As a result, there will be less and less incentive for them to see any (radical and thorough) political and economic reforms that could affect their existing benefits. Last but not least, in contrast to the reforms that had been merely decided by the political elite (including both CCP radicals and conservatives) before the mid-1990s (which have been discussed in Section 2.1 of Chapter 2), the reforms that have been decided by the political elite in cooperation with the economic and cultural elites since then have been far more limited in scope (as shown in Figure 2.1).

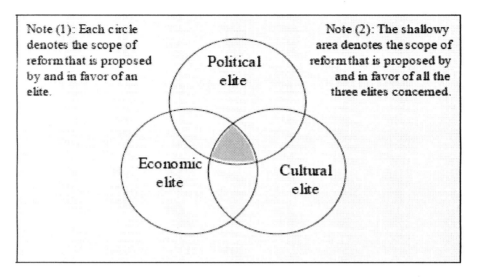

Note (1): Each circle denotes the scope of reform that is proposed by and in favor of an elite.

Note (2): The shallowy area denotes the scope of reform that is proposed by and in favor of all the three elites concerned.

Political elite

Economic elite

Cultural elite

Figure 2.1. Collective actions of the Chinese elites on reforms.

2.3. OPTIMIZING REFORM STRATEGIES: TWO GAMES

The following two games illustrate both the threat to radical economic reform and the value of the balance rule for precluding this threat. The first game is between three players: the radicals (R), the conservatives (S) and the incumbent bureaucrats (IB). The second game adds a fourth player who may veto the entire set of policies: backstage ruler (BSR). We assume that BSR holds the balance of political power between the R and S. In addition, uncertainty affects how the players view the reform strategy. To make this circumstance concrete, we assume that uncertainty concerns political stability: the country may experience either normal (political stable) times or a political crisis. Finally, we further assume:

(1) R chooses a radical ('Big bang') reform (labeled as BB) during the normal times; it chooses a gradual reform (labeled as GR) during a political crisis.[7]

(2) When R chooses BB, IB supports S; when R chooses GR, IB supports R during normal times and supports S during a political crisis.

---

[7] This assumption is based simply on the fact that all radicals have a CCP background and do not want any reforms that could lead to the collapse of the CCP-dominated nation.

(3) As defined by their very natures, R and S cannot reach an agreement concerning a reform in any circumstances, but they can compromise in the following ways: S accepts no reform (labeled as NR) when R advocates GR; and it accepts GR when R advocates BB.

(4) BSR can veto over R's BB (in case of political crisis) and S's NR (during normal times); it instead tolerates all other reforms, no matter who will lead the reforms.

To simplify the decision tree, we assume in both games that the winner implements the policy it advocated. As to the information assumptions: We assume that R must choose in ignorance of the state of political stability while IB knows and, to some extent, decides the state of political stability when it must choose between R and S. The games are a highly stylized representation of post-Mao politics.

Game 1: Reform in the absence of a BSR veto

Understanding the game's implications requires a calculation of the equilibrium outcomes. To begin this step, consider the sequence of choices made by the players. The game represents uncertainty over the society by a non-strategic player, called political status (PS), who has the first move (see Figure 2.2). With probabilities of π and $1-\pi$, PS chooses normal times and a political crisis, respectively. The move by PS represents a convenient way to express the uncertainty facing the second player, who must choose prior to knowing the state of political stability.

After PS moves, R moves and may advocate either BB or GR. The shadowed area around R's two decision nodes in Figure 2.2 indicates that R does not know the state of political stability at the time of its decision. After taking into account the characteristics of China's political evolutions, we suppose that R must choose in ignorance of the state of political stability, while IB knows and can, due to its deep influence on Chinese society, decide the state of political stability when it must choose. The outcomes are summarized as follows. If R wins BB, the outcome is A; if it wins GR, the outcome is B if IB and S do not form a coalition and is C if IB and S form a coalition. If S wins, the outcome is 'no reform' (D). The preferences of R, IB, S and BSR are given in Table 2.1.

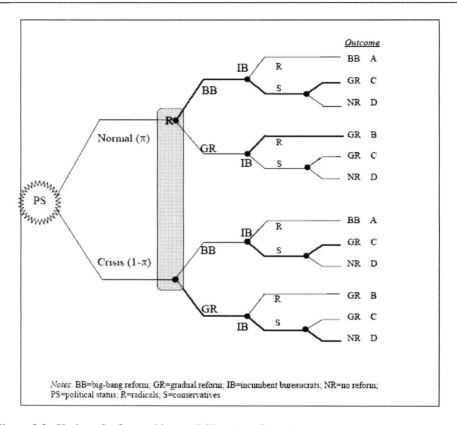

Figure 2.2. Choice of reform without a BSR veto – Game 1.

Table 2.1. Players' preference ranking

No.	Radicals (R)		Incumbent bureaucrats (IB)		Conservatives (S)	Backstage ruler (BSR)
	In normal times	In political crisis	In normal times	In political crisis		
1	A	B	B	D	D	B, C
2	B	A	D	C	C	
3	C	C	C	B	B	A, D
4	D	D	A	A	A	

Notes: (1) the reason for R to rank C after A is that in a political crisis R losses supporters in both cases it would be more likely to stake a big-bang reform (A) than to exercise a gradual reform (B); (2) the reason for IB to rank D and C after B is that in normal times, a gradual reform means more benefits rather than costs; and (3) we assume that the BSR cannot differentiate C from B and D from A, and that B and C, and A and D are equally treated by the BSR.

The IB's preferences depend on the state of political stability. During normal times, IB prefers R's gradual reform (B) to S's no reform (D). The four outcomes are ranked as follows: R's gradual reform (B) is preferred to no actions on reforms (D), which are preferred to S's gradual reform (C) and lastly, to R's 'Big bang' reform (A). During a political crisis, however, IB prefers S's policies to R's policies, ranking the four outcomes as follows: no reform (D) is preferred to S's gradual reform (C), which are preferred to R's gradual reform (B) and, lastly, to R's 'Big bang' reform (A). Regardless of the state of political stability, S ranks the outcomes as D→C→B→A, and BSR ranks the outcomes as B/C→A/D.

To determine the outcome of the game, we solve a subgame-perfect equilibrium, requiring that an action be specified for each decision-maker at each node of the game. Consider IB's choices in Figure 2.2. During normal times, if R chooses BB, IB will cooperate with S for a gradual reform (C); if R chooses GR, IB will cooperate with R for a gradual reform (B). Although the final outcomes of B and C are the same, the cost of implementing B is lower than that of implementing C, since in C there is an extra risk for reversing BB to GR. As a result, IB prefers the R-advocated gradual reform (B) to the S-advocated gradual reform (C). This leads to the following behavior by IB: during normal times, IB will cooperate with R for a gradual reform (B) if R advocates GR, otherwise IB will cooperate with S for a gradual reform (C); during a political crisis, IB will cooperate with S for a gradual reform (C) if R advocates BB, otherwise IB will cooperate with S for no reform (NR). In both cases, R will lose its power in the country during a political crisis.

IB's behavior sets the stage for R's decisions. R does not know whether there will be a political crisis. Because it does not win regardless of its decision if there is a political crisis, and because it wins during normal times only if it chooses GR, it will choose GR. In this game, S is able to attract IB in normal times if R advocates BB and in a political crisis regardless of R's choices. By contrast, R is often isolated and, without careful treatment, R is in trouble.

Game 2: Reform under a BSR Veto

The sequence of action in the second game adds an additional (fifth) move by BSR to the four moves in the first game. BSR may veto the entire set of policies (Figure 2.3), resulting in a payoff of 0 to IB and BSR. If R leads reforms, BSR prefers B to A; if S leads reforms BSR prefers C to D (see Table 2.1).

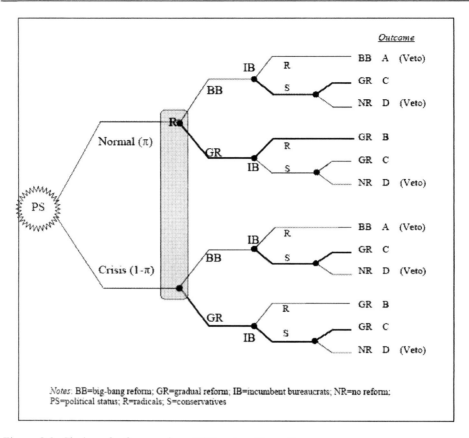

Figure 2.3. Choice of reform under a BSR veto – Game 2.

We again solve for the equilibrium by backward induction. Although this game has 24 end nodes, there are only four possible outcomes, making it relatively easier for us to solve. In the game's last move, BSR must choose between the outcome arrived at by the previous move or, by exercising its veto. Because BSR prefers 0 only to outcomes A and D, it will exercise its veto only when the previous moves yield A and D. In all other circumstances, a veto would make BSR worse off. The following contingent rule for exercising its veto summarizes BSR's behavior at its 12 decision nodes: BSR's exercises its veto if and only if R chooses BB during a political crisis and S chooses NR during normal times. This implies that BSR exercises its veto only at its first and last decision nodes (numbering the nodes from top to bottom).

Working backgward the next set of decision nodes requires a choice by S and IB, who take BSR's behavior as given. Consider normal times. If R advocates BB, it will not receive any support from IB; even worse, it will lead IB and S to form a coalition, and in addition it will face a veto by BSR since the coalition of IB and S could result in a political crisis. Therefore, R will choose GR instead of BB. If instead R advocates GR, choosing R yields outcome B, whereas choosing S yields outcome C. In both cases, IB prefers R's GR to S's. In a political crisis, IB never supports R even though the latter chooses a moderate reform strategy (GR). Choosing S yields outcome C if R advocates BB and outcome D if R advocates GR. But since S knows in advance that BSR will veto over outcome D (no reform), choosing S will yield outcome C in both cases.

Next consider R's decision at the first node. Taking IB and BSR's behavior as given, we observe that IB never chooses R during a political crisis, whereas during normal times IB chooses R if R advocates GR. R can never win by advocating BB, but it can win during normal times and if it advocates GR. So R will choose GR as long as the possibility of political stability, π, exceeds zero. In the equilibrium of this game, S will win when the relative frequency of political crisis is high ($\pi < 0.5$). In the face of a BSR veto, both R and S will temper their radical initiatives.

Game 2 demonstrates that the outcome changes when the BSR holds a veto over both R and S. Because the BSR will veto R when R attempts to implement the 'Big bang' economic reform policies, IB prefers S to R when R advocates BB. This leads to a change in R's behavior and instead it advocates only GR policy. R's behavior under balance implies that IB prefers S to R during bad times and R to S during good times. Both the radicals and the conservatives could have decided the extent of their cooperation in negotiating a mutually accepted strategy of reforms. At the same time, they could have also initiated a costly confrontation with each other so as to gain supremacy over Chinese society. This situation may be depicted as a repetitive, complete information game (Bates *et al.*, 1998, p. 30).

The analytical framework presented in this section sets out to deal with the characteristics of the set of mutual deterrence (sub-game perfect) equilibria (MDEs).[8] In such equilibria, the confrontation between the radicals and the conservatives does not occur. Concentration on these equilibria is motivated by two considerations. First, the stable and mutually accepted reforms during most, if not all of the years of the 1980s and 1990s indicates that each side of the radicals and the conservatives was indeed deterred from challenging the other. Secondly, since confrontation is costly, refraining from it was economically efficient. Furthermore, since implementing reforms was efficient, studying whether the need for the Chinese political system to be self-enforcing affected its economy is

---

[8] We borrow this term from Bates *et al.* (1998, p. 31).

to examine whether this need constrained cooperation in reaching an MDE with the efficient reform strategy (i.e., the length of time for the reforms to be completed).

Examining whether China's self-enforcing political system reached an MDE with the efficient reform strategy requires analyzing the incentives for the radicals and the conservatives to cooperate with each other. For simplicity, our analysis first examines the MDE for a given set of reform strategies; only then is it extended to allow the reforms to be determined endogenously. This approach reveals the distinct political and economic characteristics of efficient and inefficient MDEs, enabling us to compare the insights gained from the theoretical finding with the historical evidence.

To understand the implications of the incentives for the policymakers to implement reforms, the relations between the radicals and conservatives should be made explicit. For ease of analysis, we assume that: (i) the radicals prefer a 'Big bang' to gradual reform; and (ii) the conservatives do not prefer any reforms or at least prefer a gradual to big-bang reform. Since both the radicals and the conservatives can recruit supporters through their contributions to the growth of incomes, the tradeoff between them was inherent in the nature of the political exchange through which reforms were implemented.

Assume that there is a fixed length of time for the reforms to be completed, T^*, that maximizes the (gross) income for the radicals and the conservatives.[9] Hence, if the actual length of time for the reforms is shorter than that length, the income for the radicals is larger than for the conservatives; by contrast, if it is longer than that length, the income for the conservatives is larger than for the radicals.

The analysis can now be extended to examine the reform strategy in acquisition of which both the radicals and the conservatives would find it optimal to cooperate, in other words, to examine the length of time by which to implement the reforms. The analysis addresses the following question: Does the efficient MDE maximize the conservatives' incomes? If the answer to this question is affirmative, it can be concluded (at least from the static point of view) that the need to sustain China's self-enforcing political system did not theoretically entail economic cost. If the answer to this question is negative, however, it can be concluded that, theoretically, the need to sustain China's self-enforcing political system hindered economic efficiency, since the conservatives would not cooperate

---

[9] Note that if the expected length of time for the reforms is T_{BB} for the radicals and T_{GR} for the conservatives, we have $T_{BB} \leq T^* \leq T_{GR}$.

in achieving the efficient MDE. If this is the case, we can also use the model to identify the exact sources of this inefficiency.

Addressing these questions requires examining when an MDE implies an increasing numbers of supporters. If there are no reforms, this implies no gains from cooperation. Hence, in the absence of reforms, the conservatives would neither increase the incomes of their own, nor recruit supporters from the society. At the same time, since the reform could increase incomes for all sides concerned, the radicals would be able to provoke challenges if they were facing resistance from the conservatives. By contrast, incentives for the conservatives to cooperate with the radicals decrease, since each side only obtained a decreasingly marginal gain.

Let us now come to examine how external policy influences the choice of reform strategies.[10] Why did the open-door policy yield incentives for policy-makers to choose the gradual vis-à-vis big-bang reforms in China? To understand this case, one must bear in mind the characteristics of the political evolutions in China. During the 1980s and the 1990s, most political elite (especially those conservatives) still treated the open-door policy as both an economically good and a politically bad measure (we have addressed them in Figure 2.2).

This analysis has been motivated by the quest to identify the possible sources for political order in China and, specifically, by the inability of narrative to resolve two conflicting interpretations of the prevalence of economic reforms during most of the 1980s and the 1990s. Our analysis indicates that both reform strategies – gradual/partial and radical – can be correct, which depend on the internal and external environments of the Chinese economy.

2.4. CHINESE-STYLE REFORM: FUTURE PERSPECTIVE

During the twentieth century the failure of the centrally planned economies (CPEs) to keep pace with their market-oriented counterparts demonstrated quite clearly that planning entire economies at the level of central government does not offer a productive path to long-term development. Since 1978, economic reforms in China have sought to improve, among other things, enterprise incentive systems with greater relative decision-making autonomy. The dynamism of the Chinese economy may be attributed to a variety of reform measures. One such measure was the lifting of previous restrictions on the development of non-state

---

[10] Note that in Conditions 1 and 2 the optimal reform strategies have nothing to do with open-door policies.

sectors and the policy of promoting a diversified ownership structure. This has led to the explosive growth of the non-state sectors that are acting increasingly as the engine of economic development particularly since the early 1990s when China formally tried to transform its economy to a socialist market system.

The economic reforms introduced in many former CPEs followed their domestic political crises (such as the collapse of the Soviet Union in the case of Russia, and the death of Mao Zedong and the fall of the leftist 'Gang of Four' in China). However, successful reforms are also promoted by a favorable international environment. Haggard and Webb (1994) have found that international factors influence reform through a number of channels, such as the prospect of trade concessions and agreements, conditionality and ideas brought by external advisers and technocrats trained abroad. The significant role of the open-door policy in market-oriented reform can be witnessed by the Chinese experience. China's application to get access to the GATT/WTO lasted for 16 years – from 1986 to 2002. After each of the long-running negotiations, China's centrally planned system on foreign trade had a gradual reform towards the market-oriented economic system. During the 1990s, almost all major Chinese reforms on foreign trade system were marked by the WTO accession negotiations (Chi, 2000).

It is now generally believed that the Chinese outward-oriented development policy was borrowed in part from the experiences of the newly-industrialized economies (NIEs) in East Asia. On the one hand, the reformist leaders were also deeply aware that their rivals from the Chinese Civil War across the Taiwan Strait, their compatriots in colonial Hong Kong, and their Cold War enemies in southern Korea were enjoying sustained economic success that raised deeply challenging questions about China's own continuing backwardness (Garnaut, 1999, pp. 2–3). On the other hand, China and the USA saw the former Soviet Union as their common enemy and this led Mao and Nixon to normalize Sino–US relations in 1971, which paved the way for China's re-engagement with the non-communist world. Later the defeat of the US forces in Vietnam meant that the West appeared to be a less threatening place to China's leaders, facilitating China's re-entry into the global economy (Liew *et al.*, 2003).

Precisely, China's economic reform has provided fewer incentives and opportunities for provincial and local governments to make use of the comparative advantages for interregional cooperation in the 1980s than in the 1990s. The following research evidence can witness this phenomenon. Young (2000), based on the pre-1990s data, finds that China's economic reform resulted in a fragmented internal market with fiefdoms controlled by local officials whose economic and political ties to protected industry resembled those observed in

Latin American economies in previous decades. It seems plausible that the endogenous response of actors to the rent-seeking opportunities created by gradualist reform could give rise to new distortions, whose lifespan far exceeds that of the rents which had motivated their initial arrival (Young, 2000). Based on the data from 1988 to 2000, Cai *et al.* (2002), however, argue that the decentralization of authority has already generated comparative advantages for interregional cooperation in the manufacturing sector during the reform period. If both results are correct, the Chinese reform might suggest that 'Big bang' tends to be optimal in the early stage of reform and that gradualism tends to be optimal in the late stage of reform.

It is almost certain that the Chinese-style reform would not be reversed in the foreseen future. This is not only because the Chinese-style reform has become a win–win game for all who are in power, but also because it has meant that the Chinese economy is more and more dependent on the outside world. Since China's entrance into the WTO in November 2002, external stakeholders (such as international financial organizations and foreign-owned enterprises) have been increasingly influencing the Chinese economic reform. However, the collective actions of these stakeholders on the Chinese reforms are much more complicated than those of the Chinese domestic stakeholders. For example, with regard to the reform on the current exchange rate system under which the Chinese currency has been, as generally recognized, devalued, there are two different voices from the outside world. While countries having large trade deficits with China have requested that the level of the Chinese currency should be more freely determined by the market, their overseas enterprises in China have benefited significantly from this currency devaluation by exporting their made-in-China products to the outside world.

China is now faced by the dilemma of whether to follow the past tune (that is, the gradual and partial strategy) in order to minimize the risk of macroeconomic transition or to go faster in order to satisfy the WTO requirements with the fixed timetable. However, it seems that the Chinese government is not prepared to bear the potential risk of any substantial or radical reforms. One example is the reform of the foreign exchange system. As will be stated in Section 3.3 of Chapter 3, China's gradual/partial reform on foreign exchange system has contributed significantly to its robust foreign trade performance on the one hand and its domestic economic stability on the other. However, since 1994 when a unitary and floating exchange-rate system was established, there has been no substantial reform. Obviously, this system is to a large extent determined by the government; the foreign exchange rate is controlled officially and the central bank is one of the biggest participants in the market.

While China's reform has been driving its economic growth strongly, it has also produced a series of socioeconomic problems. By openly proclaiming itself a party of the 'economic elite' that has benefited from its free market agenda, the CCP has been hoping to consolidate a reliable base of support for its continued rule. With its pro-growth polices, ban on independent trade unions and low environmental standards, the CCP has created an advantageous atmosphere for the economic elite to make money. Policies so favor the rich and business that China's economic program, in the words of one Western ambassador, resembles 'the dream of the American Republican Party'.[11]

Indeed, the CCP's three represents theory clearly states that the CCP is no longer the single representative of poor, working-class people; rather, it has also been the representatives of economic and cultural elites in China. A glance at China's past social and economic transformations reveals that the large surge in income inequalities was not the only unwanted result of the Chinese-style reform. The worsening of social and political progress during the 1990s and the 2000s is another example. For example, China's score of 'control of corruption' was more than 50 in 1996 (see Figure 2.4a) but it dropped to only 30 in 2007 (see Figure 2.4c); from 1996 to 2002 its score in terms of 'voice and accountability' was among the lowest of all of the nations considered by the World Bank (see Figure 2.4b) and there is no sign of improvements from 2002 to 2007 (see Figure 2.4c). Without good reason, China's party-state political system has lacked the informational and incentive roles of democracy that, working mainly through open public discussion, could be of pivotal importance for the reach of social and public policies.

Since the beginning of its economic reform, China has benefited increasingly from global interdependence and the modern world's free flow of goods, capital and people. However, with those benefits have also come the responsibilities of accountability and transparency. China's party-state system has exposed the dearth of political dynamics. The Severe Acute Respiratory Syndrome (SARS) epidemic spread which throughout China in April 2003 exposed some of China's institutional weakness.[12]

---

[11] Cited from www.wsws.org/articles/2002/nov2002/chin-n13.shtml.

[12] From November 2002 to 2003, SARS infected over 8,000 people in 30 countries and killed more than 500. In addition to the human toll, it was inflicting significant economic damage across Asia. Besides Hong Kong, which was among the worst hit, GDP growth rates in Taiwan, Singapore and Thailand were also lower in 2003. Nowhere was SARS having more impact than on mainland China, where the disease started.

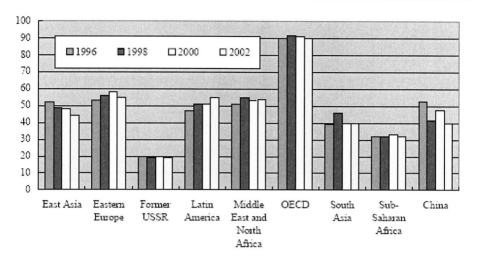

(a) Control of Corruption

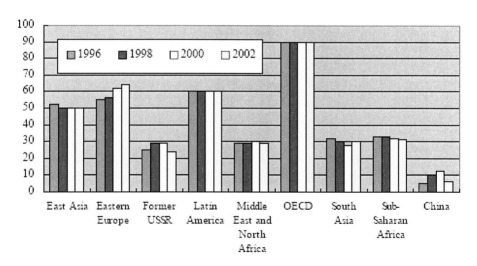

(b) Voice and Accountability

Figure 2.4. (Continued).

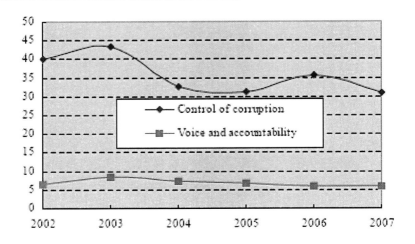

(c) China 2002–2007

Note: the y-coordinates denote the degrees of 'control of corruption' and 'voice and accountability', respectively (100=maximum level; 0=minimum level).

Source: Created by the author based on Kaufmann *et al*. (2008).

Figure 2.4. Social and political capacities, China and the world.

Yet the greatest impact of the SARS crisis may be on China's antiquated political system. Chinese mismanagement of the outbreak has plainly exposed just how far political reform has lagged behind economic development. Beijing's long concealment of the truth is exposing political faultlines by simultaneously weakening the economy, damaging the government's credibility. The crisis has undermined traditional supporters, aggravating old demographic strains, and emboldening detractors to more assertively protest government policy. While the growing pressure from a more demanding public and an increasingly interdependent world has forced China to re-evaluate its political and socioeconomic policies, the extent of any resulting political reform depend on whether the enhanced incentives for accountability and transparency among public officials override the traditional incentives for party and factional loyalty.

In short, for the majority of the past three decades, China's reform has achieved two objectives simultaneously: to improve economic efficiency by unleashing the standard forces of incentives and competition on the one hand; and to make the reform a win–win game and therefore in the interests of those in power on the other (Qian, 2002). And they take into consideration China's specific political and cultural conditions. With its impressive economic achievements, today the Chinese reform is rarely called into question. However, it still remained problematic in social and political perspectives throughout the reform era. Ironically, China's economic growth was obtained at the cost of a retardation of political reforms, not to mention worsening income inequalities as well as other social problems. As China continues to integrate with the world economy and accepts other global values, there are mounting pressures for political reform.

.

Chapter 3

A COMPARISON OF THE (UN)SUCCESSFUL CASES OF REFORM

According to the new institutional economics, system, like other production factors required in economic development, is a special kind of scarce resource and should thus be treated properly in economics. The economic system of any nation is the mechanism that brings together natural resources, labor, technology and the necessary managerial talents. Anticipating and then meeting human needs through the production and distribution of goods and services is the end purpose of every economic system. While the type of economic system applied by a nation is usually decided artificially, it is also to a large extent the result of historical experience, which becomes over time a part of political culture.

Considered a reform program consisting of two reform measures that can be carried out simultaneously or sequentially. Suppose that the economic outcome of the full reform is in most circumstances better than that of each partial reform measure.

Without considering the cost of implementation, a big bang reform may have an advantage over a gradual one.[1] However, once reforms are turned back sometimes due to the political and economic uncertainties, the reversal is more costly for the full reform than the partial one, which means reversing the full reform sometimes costs more than reversing a single partial reform measure.[2]

---

[1] Examples that support big bang reforms would include Lipton and Sachs (1990), Åslund (1991), Berg and Sachs (1992), Boycko (1992), Murphy *et al.* (1992), Sachs (1993), Frydman and Rapaczynski (1994) and Woo (1994).

[2] Examples that support gradual reforms would include Svejnar (1989), Portes (1990), McKinnon (1991b), Roland (1991), Dewatripont and Roland (1992a, 1992b, and 1995), McMillan and Naughton (1992), Murrell (1992), Aghion and Blanchard (1994), Litwack and Qian (1998) and Wei (1993).

In the chapter, we will examine and compare various successful and unsuccessful cases of the Chinese-style reform. It should be noted that the judgment of a reform as being 'successful' or 'unsuccessful' is based on some available data and literature. Frankly speaking, there is no mandatory standard for this definition since each reform – no matter whether not it has been 'successful' ('unsuccessful') – has both positive and negative effects on the Chinese economy. In addition, the terms 'radical' and 'gradual/partial' reforms used in these sections are also defined elastically, since judged by international standards, over the course of the past three decades China's reforms as a whole have been implemented via only but a gradual/partial approach.

3.1. RADICAL REFORM, THE SUCCESSFUL CASES

China's agricultural reforms began in September 1980 and had been completed successfully before the end of 1982. The CCP and the Chinese government took only about two years to decollectivize about 700 million farmers throughout the huge nation, through a method known as household responsibility system (HRS). Under the HRS, each household may be able to sign a contract with the local government and then obtain a certain amount of arable land and production equipment depending on the number of rural population in this family and have a production quota. As long as the household completes its quota of products to the state, it can decide freely what to produce and how to sell. Although land is still owned by the state, the incentive for agricultural production has increased significantly. The decollectivization of agriculture, which has been recognized as a radical reform (Sachs and Woo, 1994; and Zhao, 1999, p. 192), has universally been recognized as a success. For example, from 1978 to 1984, grain output increased by 56 percent (Lin, 1992). Even more rapid was the growth in the output of other agricultural commodities (during the pre-reform period, the growth in grain output had been at the expense of these commodities). Over the longer period of reform from 1978 to 2002, gross agricultural output had grown in real terms at an average annual rate of more than 5 percent (NBS, 2003).

The special political and economic features of China determine the driving forces and the outcomes of the reform in agricultural ownership. First, more than 80 percent of China's population still lived in 1978 in rural areas – a backward and autarky society.[3] Secondly, China's agricultural sector had been dominated by collectivist ownership before the reform – which did not fit a standard socialist model. As a result, reforming the collective sector (while keeping the state-owned sector unchanged) would not have been regarded by the conservatives as fundamentally affecting China's socialist orthodoxy. Thirdly, and most importantly, the Chinese policymakers – from both reformist and conservative cliques – still had remembered the three-year famine (1959–61) during which millions of farmers died of starvation. They should have recognized that the horrible famine had attributed to, at least partially, China's highly centralized agricultural system, and that if it would occur again, the CCP would lose its power base in China.

Since the initial and external conditions of the agricultural sector were similar to those of the industrial sector (especially those of the small state-owned and collectively-owned industrial enterprises), we argue that at least some of the industrial reforms – which had followed a too gradual/partial pace (as will be discussed in Section 3.4 of Chapter 3) – were misguided during the early 1980s. Had the industrial reform followed a more radical approach in terms of speed and scope during the early stage of reform, there would have been more positive economic performances in the industrial sector.

Another successful case relates to the reform of Chinese bureaucracy. The first task undertaken by Deng Xiaoping after he resumed his job was to reform the bureaucratic institutions. Manned by millions of workers, the system was acknowledged officially to be overstaffed and sluggish. The drive to weed out tens of thousands of aged, inactive and incompetent personnel was intensified. Even more revolutionary, the life tenure system for state and party cadres was abolished, and age limits for various offices were established and, on a less restrictive basis, an education requirement for each level of government positions (see Table 3.1 for a summary of the reform). While removing superfluous personnel, the reform leaders stressed the importance of creating a 'third echelon' of younger leadership to enter responsible positions and be trained for future authority.

The major and direct consequence of the bureaucratic reform is that many younger and better-educated bureaucrats have replaced the older revolutionary veterans. The new, younger officials were generally more supportive of the government reforms, as well as being more adaptable and more pragmatic.

---

[3] Note that as a result of three decades of effective CCP control on the one hand and of the closed-door policy on the other, most, if not all peasants in rural China had been accustomed to obeying political and economic orders coming from Beijing.

Table 3.1. Chinese bureaucratic reform, Feb. 1982 to Sept. 1984

Statistic	Provincial governors	Ministers	City mayors or department chiefs	County sheriffs or division chiefs
Mandatory retirement age (years)	65	65	60	55
Average retirement age (years) −Before reform −After reform	62 55	64 58	58 50	- <45
Percentage with college degree (%) −Before reform −After reform	20 43	37 52	14 44	11 45
Average tenure (years) −Pre-1982 −Post-1982	6.43/6.23[a] 3.84/4.05[a]	6.56 4.44	- -	- -

Notes: By 1988, 90% of government officials above the country level were newly appointed after 1982; 60% of those government officials had college degrees. This was a result of retiring 3.4 million revolutionary veterans. [a]: Governor/party secretary.

Source: Li (1998, p. 394), which also gives other references.

Being better educated in almost all cases, they were also generally more competent than their predecessors (Li, 1998, p. 394). Clearly, the Chinese-style reform of bureaucracy served as a stable political foundation for the implementation of the economic reform during the past decades. Without that reform, in which more younger cadres were able to play an important role, the afterwards reforms would have been impossible.

Although the two reforms outlined above have been regarded as successful cases, they also had some negative effects. For example, the cooperative medical care system, which had worked quite well before the reform in rural areas, was abandoned as a result of the household responsibility system (HRS). [4] The implementation of the policy of 'buying-out' the ageing bureaucrats also had some negative effects. An implicit and informal arrangement for most senior officials was that their children were allowed to enter politics in senior positions, which resulted in the birth of the infamous *taizhidang* (party of crown prince) in

---

[4] For example, according to a World Bank report, before reform, China's "barefoot doctor" approach in its rural areas had been an important model for primary health care worldwide (Hammer, 1995).

China. It is worth noting that the rise of the *taizidang* often happened in parallel with political and economic corruption. However, the above problems were not because the reforms were too radical but that they were too mild (especially in the case of bureaucratic reform) and limited in scope (especially in the case of agricultural reform).

3.2. RADICAL REFORM, THE UNSUCCESSFUL CASES

After nearly ten years of reforms and debates over the relative merits of plan and market, a radical price reform was introduced suddenly in June 1998. This was based on the idea that 'long pain is not better than short pain', and that market prices should be put in place at once.

Theoretically, if price subsidies are a significant cause for deficits and if supply is highly elastic then fiscal stabilization calls for early and speedy price liberalization (Liew *et al.*, 2003). According to this theory, the greater the fiscal deficits (if they are not due to price subsidies) and the value of forced savings and the smaller the supply elasticities, the longer should be the lag between fiscal and monetary stabilization and price liberalization. The macroeconomic environment was not favorable to the implementation of any such radical price reforms: the level of inflation was very high (18.5 percent in 1988) and friction from dual pricing was at its worst (for example, the planned price for steel was 700 yuan per ton while the market price was 1,800 yuan per ton) (Zhao, 1999, p. 195). From 1985 to 1988, the level of price subsidies increased (Jin *et al.*, 2001), as did the fiscal deficit stemming from it. The supply was constrained as a result of the decreasing marginal return from the early reform in agricultural sector on the one hand, and the unsuccessful reform in state-owned industrial sector (as will be discussed in Section 3.4 of Chapter 3) on the other. Implementing the price reform under these circumstances was both politically and socially impractical in China.[5]

Another notable case concerned China's various attempts to achieve radical SOE reform during the late 1980s and the 1990s. This had been delayed on several occasions, due to the serious concerns about the social instability that might result from the reform. The SOE reform is sufficiently extensive to cause large increases in unemployment. In December 1986, the 'Bankruptcy Law Concerning the SOEs' was adopted by the NPC. However, the law was not

---

[5] I still remember that, upon hearing the news about price reform in August 1988, I rushed to an electrical appliances shop to buy a radio-recorder, which was worthy of my ten-month salary but seldom used in the following years.

effectively applied until 1994 due to fears of unemployment and social instability, as China had only relatively primitive social security system.

The reform on non-performing SOEs was debated once again in the Fifth Plenum of the Fourteenth CCPCC held during September 1995. The outcome was the policy of 'grasping the large and releasing the small'. To 'grasp the large' (zhuada) is to turn a select group of 300 out of a list of 1,000 already successful large enterprises and enterprise groups into world-class businesses. To 'release the small' (fangxiao) is to privatize or to contract out small SOEs or to allow them to go bankrupt. This policy allows most small SOEs to be sold off to private individuals; the management of those not sold is contracted out (Liew, 1999, p. 93). During the first two years, when the government began to release small and non-performing SOEs and to lay off superfluous workers, there was serious resistance to these reforms.

Notice that since the mid-1990s the CCP and the central government have been particularly concerned about the increasing number of illegal organizations established to organize protests against the radical SOE reform (see the final paragraph of Section 3.4 of Chapter 3 for detailed evidence). This can be found, for example, in Jiang Zemin's speech at the meeting commemorating the twentieth anniversary of the Third Plenum of the Eleventh CCP National Congress (Jiang, 1998, p. 2). In contrast to the Western democratic countries in which protests against government can be found regularly, the protests were unusual in the PRC's history, especially during the post-reform period. They could easily remind the CCP and central government of the Tian'anmen incident in June 1989. Consequently, they could retard any further efforts on the radical reforms of the SOEs.

We are not able to verify if – or to what extent – the SOE reform, if it had been implemented earlier, could have been more successful. But, arguably, if the substantial ownership reform of the small and rural-based SOEs were introduced in parallel with or immediately following the radical agricultural ownership reform during the early stages (that is, in the late 1970s or the early 1980s), there would have been similar, positive economic performances. The primary reason lies in the fact that the market culture based on private ownership – the main form of ownership before the 1950s – still remained a memory of most middle-aged SOE workers in China in the early 1980s. The critical role that the retired SOE workers played in the dramatic growth of the township and village-based enterprises (McMillan and Naughton, 1992; and World Bank, 1996, p. 51) indicates that the SOEs and the SOE workers could become more productive if the property right and incentive system moved away from the model of state ownership.

3.3. GRADUAL/PARTIAL REFORM, THE SUCCESSFUL CASES

The key component of China's gradual/partial reform was the introduction of a dual-track system, which was implemented first in agricultural products, before spreading slowly to consumer goods and intermediate goods. In each case, a free market in which the price was subject to the market regulations developed in parallel with a controlled market in which the price was kept almost unchanged at an officially fixed level. Because the price was higher in the market-regulated track than in the state-controlled track, supply in the free market grew rapidly, so that its share in total output rose steadily. Meanwhile, the planned price was able to rise incrementally until it approached the market price when there was a narrowing of the gap between supply and demand.

The dual-track system extended through almost every sphere of the Chinese economy, from agriculture, industry, commerce, transportation, post and telecommunications to health care, education and so on during the transition. For example, between 1979 and 1992, the proportion of industrial goods and materials distributed under the central plan system declined from 95 percent to less than 10 percent. There was a parallel reduction in the planned allocation of consumer goods: the number of first-class goods distributed by the state dropped from 65 to 20 and that of the production of materials distributed by the state was reduced from 256 to 19 during the period (Liu, 1995, p. 53).

The smooth implementation of the dual-track system depended on the material compensation of and the spiritual consolation for various losers. For example, although consumers have been able to buy foodstuffs on the free market since 1980, urban food coupons (for purchasing grain, meat, oil and so on) were finally removed only in the early 1990s. Guangzhou completed the removal of the above coupons in 1992 and spent on average 103 yuan in 1988, 113 yuan in 1990, and 43 yuan in 1992 per urban resident for compensation. Beijing also spent 182 yuan in 1990, 185 yuan in 1991, and 123 yuan in 1994 per head before its removal of the coupons (Qian, 2002). In addition, when the reformists decided to reduce the share of centrally planned economy during the 1980s, spiritual consolation also applied to the conservatives who had strongly believed that the Chinese economy must be regulated mainly by planning and supplementally by the market mechanism. This can be illustrated in more details below.

During the 1980s there had been extensive and heated arguments about how plan and market could be appropriately combined in the Chinese economy. While the CCP conservatives strongly believed that the Chinese economy should be regulated mainly by planning and supplementally by market, some economists advocating laissez-faire suggested an increasing share of market regulation. In order to resolve this dispute, Chinese reformists invented a term – 'guided plan'. Compared to 'commanded plan' (under which both the price and the quantity of each commodity are strictly controlled by the central government), 'guided plan' only relates to those that are under the loose control of the central or local government. It is interesting to note that the definition of the term 'guided plan' is quite fuzzy. In practice, commodities under the 'guided plan' scheme can be treated either as part of those regulated by 'plan' or as part of those regulated by 'market' (see Figure 3.1). What the reformists intended to do was to, while not violating the principle of "regulation mainly by planning', move Line B closer to Line A so as to reduce the scope of the 'commanded plan' (Zhao, 1998). Even though the conservatives still wanted to move Line B closer to Line C in order to retain a larger portion of purely commanded plan for the Chinese economy, confrontations between the reformists and conservatives were reduced substantially.

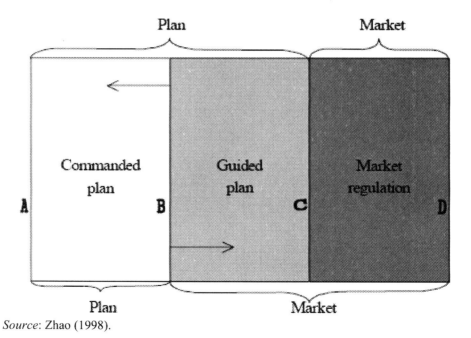

Source: Zhao (1998).

Figure 3.1. The art of reforming a centrally planned economy.

In short, a brief review of the gradually declining trend of the plan track throughout the 1980s provides evidence that, ex post, there is no 'ratcheting up' of the plan. Moreover, recent data reveal that the plan track in the product market has been largely 'phased out' in the 1990s, and that this phasing out of the plan track was accompanied in general by explicit compensation.

With rapid growth, the plan track becomes, in no time, a matter of little consequence to most potential losers, which in turn reduces the cost required for compensating them (Lau *et al.*, 2000, p. 142).

In general, the dual-track reform has been recognized as of success, since it not only avoided output declining but also improved the level of efficiency (Wu and Zhao, 1987; and Li, 1997). It must be noted that the dual-track system did not always work well, especially when a large gap existed between market-regulated and officially fixed prices (we will discuss this point later).

Another key initiative of China's gradual reform was the decentralization of authority, that is, transferring economic management and decision-making from central government to the provincial and local governments. How did the reform work in practice, and to what extent had the provincial governments' fiscal incentives been strengthened as a result of this reform? Jin *et al.* (2001), based on the panel data of 28 provinces between 1982 and 1992, find that the marginal fiscal incentives of provincial governments increased during the reform period between 1982 and 1992, compared with those during the pre-reform period from 1970 to 1979. A comparison of these findings with parallel investigations in Russia is also revealing. Zhuravskaya (2000) examined the fiscal incentives of city governments in the region–city fiscal relationship in post-reform Russia (in which the city is one level below the region, which in turn is one level below the federal government). Using the data from 35 cities for the period 1992–97, she found that increases in a city's own revenue were almost entirely offset by decreases in shared revenues from the region to the city.[6]

China's foreign exchange system used to be controlled strictly by the central government. Yet since China started its economic reform in the late 1970s, the foreign trade system has been liberalized gradually. In the early 1980s, Chinese currency RMB was non-convertible and the foreign exchanges were strictly supervised by the state. Two exchange rates were in operation during that period: an official rate published by the government and another special one for foreign trade. Such a system was aimed to enhance the country's exports and to restrict its imports, for China suffered from a serious lack of foreign exchange at that time. In 1984, as a result of improved performances in foreign trade and the economy as a whole, the government adopted a new policy of exchange retention. This policy allowed domestic enterprises and institutions to retain some of their foreign

---

[6] The resulting near-zero incentives in post-reform Russia look similar to the pre-reform China but stand in sharp contrast to the post-reform China (Qian, 2002).

currency earnings, in contrast to the previous one in which these units turned over all of their foreign currency earnings to the state. Although a larger proportion of foreign exchanges was still under the control of the government, the new retaining policy stimulated domestic enterprises to increase their exports, and hence there was a significant improvement in China's foreign trade performance. However, this kind of gradual/partial reform, together with other gradual and partial reforms on the external economic sectors, has also faced difficulties, as will be discussed in detail in Section 3.4 of Chapter 3.

3.4. GRADUAL/PARTIAL REFORM, THE UNSUCCESSFUL CASES

The evidence shows not all gradual/partial reforms have performed well in China. Among the most typical unsuccessful examples were the introduction of the responsibility system and the contract system in the SOEs in 1983 and 1986, respectively. These reforms had some positive impacts on SOEs' performance, but overall they still did not achieve the objective of turning SOEs into efficient enterprises.

In brief, there are at least the following problems for this system. First, the operating mechanism of the contract system strengthened the vertical one-to-one bargaining relationship between government and firm. It did not strengthen the competitive horizontal relationship between firms, and therefore was not consistent with market-oriented reform (Zhao, 1999, p. 196). Secondly, it did not guarantee that the SOEs became independent economic identities. Last but not least, the contract did not solve the long-term behavioral problems of the managers and employees. Their behavior was still driven by short-term motivations, impinging on the interests of the owner, the state, and damaging firms' long-term development (Huang, 1999, p. 103).

To understand the characteristics of the Chinese-style reform, one must keep in mind two important facts: first, China's vast territorial size and wide diversity in physical environments have inevitably resulted in great differences in regional economic conditions; secondly, with China's 1.3 billion population and 56 ethnic groups, most provinces, which are equivalent to a medium-sized country in the rest of the world, are considerable political and economic systems in their own right. The differences between these provinces have long been a defining characteristic of China's politics since in most instances their boundaries have been created more than two thousand years ago (Gottmann, 1973; Goodman,

1997). Furthermore, Chinese culture is not homogeneous across provinces, in terms of ethnic and linguistic groups as well as provincial politics. As a result, the chances of the adoption of a common standard and interprovincial coordination between different groups of people are not likely to be enhanced if there are markedly differing religious beliefs and cultural values.

The Chinese-style decentralization of economic authority (as discussed in Section 3.3 of Chapter 3) did not always work well, especially during the early stages of reform. Since the advent of administrative decentralization, China's national economy had become effectively 'cellularized' into a plethora of semi-autarkic regional enclaves during the 1980s. In order to protect local market and revenue sources, it became common practice in China that provinces restrict import (export) from (to) other provinces by levying high, if informal taxes on commodities and by creating non-tariff barriers. Xinjiang autonomous region, for example, effectively banned the import of 48 commodities on the grounds that they would harm its domestic economy. Jilin refused to market beer produced in its neighboring provinces of Heilongjiang and Liaoning. Hunan province prohibited exporting grain to its neighbor, Guangdong province. ... In some provinces, local authorities established, and provided finance for, a variety of schemes in order to promote the sales of local products. Enterprises from other provinces, however, often had difficulties in finding office spaces, accommodation, or land for their business activities.[7]

Another case is the reform of China's banking system, which is generally recognized to lag well behind China's dramatic moves towards a market economy that is so evident in other sectors. Prior to the beginning of reforms in 1983, the People's Bank of China (PBC), China's central bank, dominated the country's highly centralized financial scene. Not only did it control the money supply; it also managed all banking and savings activities. In effect, before the reforms the PBC was only the accounting department of the Chinese central government. At the end of 1993, the State Council issued a new plan to spur changes in the monetary and financial system that would strengthen the PBC's grip on the macroeconomic environment, create specialized banks to serve priority sectors, and push the other banks towards becoming true commercial banks. The overall objective was to separate monetary policy from normal banking functions and to convert most banks into truly independent financial entities. However, the PBC remains subservient to the finance ministry and thus cannot refuse to finance government expenditures. Branches of the PBC in the provinces and districts are also subject to the dictates of both PBC and local government officials. As a

---

[7] More detailed analysis can be found in Shen and Dai (1990), Li (1993) and Wedeman (1993).

result, it is very difficult for them to refuse loans to local government entities that demand more and more credit (Xu, 1995).

In the late 1990s, the Asian financial crisis served a very useful function: it alerted Chinese leaders to the dangers of a weak financial system. Aware of the lessons drawn from the Asian financial crisis, China wanted to quicken the pace of banking reform in 1998. The major measure was that ¥270 billion (US$33 billion) in special bonds issued in 1998 so as to recapitalize the state banks. Then in 1999, it created an asset-management company (AMC) for each of the big four state banks. The AMCs received ¥400 billion (US$48 billion) in seed capital from the Ministry of Finance (MOF) and issued ¥1 trillion (US$121 billion) worth of MOF-guaranteed bonds. They then used these funds to buy ¥1.4 trillion (US$170 billion) of bad loans from the state banks at face value. But the program has failed to cure the banks' woes, since other relevant financial and economic reforms had not been implemented. Since 1998, the percentage of bad loans on the banks' books has not fallen much, and the AMCs have had limited success in recovering or selling off the bad assets. Meanwhile, corporate governance, transparency and risk management at the state banks have only shown slight improvement (Lo, 2004).

China's gradual/partial open-door policy has serious implications for its legal system and its lack of transparency, and problems of assimilating a non-market economy.[8] For example, about 220 Chinese laws that are incompatible with WTO rules have to be changed (Reti, 2001). Furthermore, in accordance with the requirements of the WTO, banks, insurance companies, telecommunications and other service industries of the rest of the world will be allowed to operate in China according to the negotiated timetable. The impact may eventually break up the status of monopoly and state control that have existed in China for around half a century. The new bank reforms starting on 1 December 2003, opening the sector further to foreign competition, have still been too mild and limited in scope. Pressing banking and financial reforms are needed in the years to come.

3.5. CONCLUDING REMARKS

The ultimate goal of any economic system is the allocation of scarce resources among competing factions. To accomplish this goal, the economic system must deal explicitly with the supply and demand of goods and services as

---

[8] Discussions in this regard would include, for example, Garnaut and Huang (1995), Corbet (1996), Keidel (1995), Wu (1996), Mastel (1996, 1998) and Morici (1997).

well as the interaction between the two. The Chinese economy is no exception to this rule. This chapter explores the elements underpinning the design and implementation of the Chinese economic reform from 1978 onwards. It provides an explanation for the causes and timing of the major reform programs, as well as for how the success and failure of the reform efforts were associated with the initial conditions and the reform strategies.

The importance of initial conditions and strategies for economic reforms has been noted (Fischer and Gelb, 1991; and De Melo *et al.*, 1997). The question of how such issues affect the final results of economic reforms, however, still remain unresolved (Campos and Coricelli, 2002, p. 828). When considering the remarkable differences between the reforms pursued in China and Russia, one must not overlook the initial institutional conditions in each of the countries. Prior to reform, the central planning system in China lasted only a relatively short period of time (that is, from the late 1950s to the late 1970s) compared to that in the former Soviet Union (FSU) (that is, from the early twentieth century to the late 1980s). As a result, the capitalist ideology and market culture still had a strong base in China vis-à-vis the FSU.[9]

The analytical narrative of the political economic events shows (see Table 3.2 for a qualitative comparison of major reform programs) that the efficiency of China's reform depended upon: (i) the initial institutional conditions; (ii) the external environment; and (iii) the reform strategy. We argue that a radical reform tends to be more efficient than a gradual/partial one during the early stages (the late 1970s and the early 1980s), while a gradual/partial reform tends to be more efficient than a radical one in the later stages. Finally, we find that between 1978 and 2008 Chinese-style reform has evolved from the collusion of the CCP radicals and conservatives to that of the political, economic and cultural elites, at the cost of sacrificing the benefits of the rest of the people.

In comparison to those introduced in Eastern Europe and the former Soviet Union, the reforms in China have some distinctive characteristics. First, the degree to which the economic system derived from the former Soviet Union exerted an influence on the Chinese economy varied from sector to sector. The sector that was most affected was the industrialized sector of the national economy, while there was less influence on the disaggregated agricultural sector and small industries. Secondly, the economic reforms in China started at a time when China was regarded as a quasi-militaristic model of communism (Zhao,

---

[9] With regard to the FSU's relatively weakness of the market economy, Mikhail Gorbachev's speech on 11 September 1990 might be revealing: 'Our brains just could not handle this idea of a market.' Cited in Hwang (1993, p. 147).

1999, p. 186), which was different to the patterns of reforms in Eastern Europe. Thirdly, the economic reform in China preceded political reform.

Table 3.2. A comparison of selected reform programs

Strategy	Successful cases[a]	Unsuccessful cases[a]
Gradual/partial approach[b]	Dual-pricing system reform (1979–92); foreign exchange system reform (1984–)	Industrial contract system (1983; 1986); administrative decentralization (1980s – early 1990s); banking reform (1983–)
Radical approach[b]	Agricultural reform (1980–82); bureaucratic reform (1982–84)	Price-release reform (1988-89); SOE ownership reform (1980s; 1990s)

Notes: ([a]) The judgment of a reform program as being 'successful' or 'unsuccessful' is based on available data and literature. ([b]) The terms 'radical' and 'gradual/partial' are elastically defined, since according to international standard, during the past two decades China's all reform programs as a whole have been implemented via only but a gradual/partial approach.

Except for a few cases in which reform followed an approach similar to that of the 'Big bang', most Chinese economic reforms can be identified as being gradualist in nature. The Chinese-type reform introduced since 1978 has exhibited remarkable results to date. Particularly praiseworthy are the facts that the Chinese-type reform has avoided the collapse in output that is characteristic of transitions in other former centrally planned economies and that it has generated unprecedented increases in the level of living standards across the country. Over the course of the past three decades, China has successfully transformed its centrally planned system and, in particular, has achieved a faster economic growth than any other socialist or former socialist countries in the world. However, China's unusual reform experience might not be generalizable to other transition economies, since it has been shaped by a set of unique initial conditions. A particularly intriguing and understudied factor is the legacy of the Great Famine (1959–61) and of the notorious Cultural Revolution (1966–76), two major events that not only boosted Deng Xiaoping's credibility and authority as a reformer, but also laid a foundation for the smooth implementation of agricultural and bureaucratic reforms.

Chapter 4

A TALE OF TWO STATE-OWNED ENTERPRISES IN TRANSITION

4.1. BACKGROUND REVIEW[1]

After the introduction of economic reform China experienced rapid economic growth, accompanied by increased income levels. Prior to the reform, China was an egalitarian society in terms of income distribution. In the initial stage of the reform, the policy of 'letting some people get rich first' was adopted to overcome egalitarianism in income distribution, to promote efficiency with strong incentives and ultimately to realize common prosperity based on an enlarged pie. But this policy has quickly increased income gaps between different groups of people. Compared with other countries, China's Gini coefficients have been very high, only being lower than those of a few of nations in Latin America and Africa.

While China's reform has been a strong driver of its economic growth, it has also derived a series of socioeconomic problems. However, the level of income inequality has also increased dramatically during recent decades and the reduction in poverty is still a challengeable task in China. China's income inequality can be decomposed further into various components associated with provincial components and their determinants in turn identified. An analysis of within-country inequality can reveal the effects of openness, marketization, convergence due to factor mobility, and may also indicate regional polarization. Furthermore, it is important to consider heterogeneity in income inequality in both level and development over time, as well as different characteristics of sub-group dimensions.

---

[1] This chapter is based on a paper published in Chinese (Guo, Li and Xing, 2003).

In September 2001 and March 2002, and requested by the Development Research Center of the State Council and by the State Development and Reform Commission, respectively, we conducted two field surveys of these two companies.[2] Our goals are: (i) to assess how well the ownership reform performed in the state-owned enterprises (SOEs); and (ii) to clarify the relationships between ownership reform, output growth and the distribution of earnings within the SOEs. The following is a typical case of two SOEs in point.

Located in Shandong province, the Zibo Mining Group (ZBM) is a large conglomerate which has been in operation for more than one hundred years. It has therefore experienced every stage of China's political and economic transformations during the twentieth century. After the 1970s, the ZBM entered into serious recessions; until 1996, it had operated with deficits for a continuous period of 24 years. At the end of June 2001, the ZBM had a total number of 36,447 registered staff, along with 25,922 retired personnel and 10,198 dependents of deceased members of staff. It had 4.249 billion yuan of fixed assets and 3.325 billion yuan of debts, with a debt/asset ratio of 78.25 percent. During the late twentieth century, the ZBM had for a long time been treated as one of 36 worst performing SOEs in China.

In September 1995, the State Council put forward a series of guidelines on the reforms of SOEs. Based on the opinions of the Ministry of Coal Industry (MCI) concerning the reconstructions of SOEs as shareholding and partnership companies (MCI, 1997), the ZBM decided to introduce ownership reforms in its two money-losing subsidiary companies (Guangzheng and Chuangda) in 1997 and the fall of 1999, respectively. Following the reforms in ownership, both companies were able to make profits in 2001.

Guangzheng company, formerly called the Shigu coalmine, is located at Chawang township, Zichuan district. The coalmine was initially established by the Japanese in 1921 and was reconstructed by the ZBM in March 1958 and went into operation on 29 September 1960, and achieving an annual production capacity of 250,000 tons of raw coal. Restricted by the complicated geological and hydrological conditions, the coalmine produced only a total amount of 8.1 million tons of raw coal between 1960 and 1990. As a result, its operations had been based on the subsidies from the central government, with a highest annual deficit of 13.0 million yuan, before 1996. After ownership reform was finalized in 1997, Guangzheng's staff held about 90 percent of its total shares, with the capacities of producing 40,000 tons of bauxite, 20,000 tons of aluminum sulfate,

---

[2] The team members involved in the two field surveys are Zhao Renwei, Li Shi, He Dingchao, Zhao Gongzheng, Zhang Yong, Zhu Shumiao, Xing Youqiang, Wang Xiaoping, Xie Yanhong and myself.

300 tons of FRP composite materials, 300 tons of special refractory kiln furniture, as well as such non-coal production sites as cement structures, waste bricks, rock wool, springs and mechanical processing. By 2001, Guangzheng had been composed of Aluminum-Chemical Company, Special-Resistant Furniture Company, Support Plant, Garment Factory, Gasoline Stations, Printing House, Savings Branch, Building Team, Auto Repair Factory, Spring Plant, Youbang (friendly) Company, Sulfuric Acid Plant, Haitian Hotel, the Electrical and Mechanical Engineering Company, and Xingwu Grinding Wheel Factory. It successfully transformed from a single coal producer to one capable of manufacturing dozens of labor- and capital-intensive goods, with a total number of 2,150 registered staff.

Chuangda company, also formerly a coalmine with the name of Hongshan, is located at the town in Luocun, Zichuan district. The coalmine, initially established by the Germans in 1904, was occupied by the Japanese in 1914 after Germany was defeated by Japan in China during World War I. In 1953 the Hongshan coalmine was incorporated with the ZBM. From 1949 to 1990, the coalmine produced 36.27 million tons of raw coal, with a highest output of 2.24 million tons in 1960. As a result of the exhaustion of coal resources, the coalmine was closed in 1996. Facing increasingly worsening performances in coal production, the coalmine experimented with a three-year contract system and between 1987 and 1989 it introduced a series of reforms on wages. This experiment, although not entirely successful, provided some experience for the later reforms in the late 1990s.

Following the corporate reconstruction (its name was changed from Hongshan coalmine to the Chuangda company) in 1996, the state-ownership was changed to the one entitled shareholding partnership in 1999, with 90 percent of its total shares being held by the company's staff. As of the end of 2001, the Chuangda company was composed of 15 independent sub-companies (including Wire Products Company, Gypsum Building Materials Company, Aluminum and Chemical company, Rubber Company, and Machinery manufacturing Company) and other economic units, with a total number of 1,785 registered staff.

In brief, during the late 1990s and the early 2000s, the Guangzheng and the Chuangda companies went through a process of dual transformations – structural change in production and ownership reform. How have these transformations influenced the system of earnings distribution and its outcomes within each company?

4.2. THE SAMPLE SELECTION

In this research, for the year 2001, we collected the samples of 391 and 446 workers from Guangzheng and Chuangda companies, respectively. The principle of the sample collection is that we try to include workers from all age groups, sex, educational backgrounds and positions. In addition, in order to differentiate the performances between the pre- and post-reform period, we include two years: 1997 (representing the pre-reform year) and 2001 (representing the post-reform year).

For Guangzheng and Chuangda companies in the year 1997, the samples are 249 and 415 workers, respectively. Since some information or data on age, educational background, or position were lost, the number of effective samples will be reduced accordingly.

Table 4.1 shows the basic status of workers in the two companies. In 1997, the average levels of ages in Guangzheng and Chuangda companies were 32.14 and 38.85 years, respectively. This difference mainly stems from that Guangzheng's workers with 31–40 years old accounted for more than 50 percent, while in Chuangda workers with 41–50 years old are the majority. From Table 4.1 we can also observe that, in 2001, the average level of ages rose to 35.71 years in Guangzheng company and to 41.39 years in Chuangda company. This suggests that, from 1997 to 2001, the data on the samples selected from two companies are comparable.

Workers with 'junior-high school education' encompass the majority in both companies, while there are only a few of workers with 'college education'. However, over the course of the years from 1997 to 2001 Guangzheng company have filled its vacancies with more 'college graduates'; by contrast, there was a reduction in the proportion of workers with 'college graduates' in Chuangda company during the same period of time.

Occupational structures also differ between the two companies, which are mainly reflected by the proportions of technical and ordinal workers. As for the year 2001, the proportion of technical workers in Guangzheng company is 14 percentage points higher than that in Chuangda company, and, accordingly, the proportion of ordinal workers in the former is nearly 8 percentage points lower than that in the latter. It is notable that ownership does not have a substantial influence on the occupational structure, especially in Guangzheng company.

Table 4.1. About the samples

		Guangzheng		Chuangda	
		1997	2001	1997[a]	2001
	Samples (persone)	249	391	415(36)	446
	Female (%)	50.4[b]	42.0[c]	32.2[d](30.6)	34.5[e]
Age group	Average age (years)	32.14[b]	35.71[f]	38.85[g](37.06)	41.39[h]
	20 year or younger	0.0	3.6	1.0(5.6)	0.9
	21–30 years	47.5	16.3	11.1(13.9)	9.2
	31–40 years	41	54.5	42.0(41.7)	26.6
	41–50 years	11.5	23.8	45.7(38.9)	53.7
	50 years or older	0.0	1.8	0.2(0.0)	9.6
Education(%)	Average length (years)	8.44[b]	8.59[i]	10.58[j](10.86)	8.50[k]
	Primary	1.2	3.1	0.5(0.0)	0.4
	Junior high school	40.2	55.0	62.8(5.6)	57.6
	Senior high or technical school	12.0	22.0	28.8(55.6)	32.6
	College (3 and 4 years)	2.4	4.6	7.9(38.9)	7.2
	Others	44.2	15.3	0.0(0.0)	2.2
Position	High-rank staff[e]	0.7	1.2	1.7(13.9)	1.6
	Middle-rank staff	3.7	3.7	8.4(50.0)	7.8
	Office workers	3.0	4.3	4.7(27.8)	5.9
	Technical workers	24.4	22.4	4.7(0.0)	8.7
	Physical workers	68.1	68.3	80.5(8.3)	76.0

[a]: figures within parentheses are only those with data on wages; [b]: with a sample of 139 persons; [c]: with a sample of 333 persons; [d]: with a sample of 407 persons: with a sample of 438 persons [f]: with a sample of 332 persons; [g]: with a sample of 405 persons; [h]: with a sample of 436 persons; [i]: with a sample of 331 persons; [j]: with a sample of 406 persons; [k]: with a sample of 437 persons; [l]: with samples of 406 persons (1997) and of 437 persons (2001) for Chuangda. (2) Data on education (in years) are calculated based on *Zichuan Annuals* (1990).

4.3. CHANGES IN THE DISTRIBUTION OF EARNINGS

From 1997 to 2001, the distributional policies of earnings underwent significant changes in both companies. In Guangzheng company 11 kinds of wage distribution policies were established: these included "contracted wages for fixed posts", "floating wages according to profit", functional wages of posts", "wages taking a percentage of profits", "awards based on the ratios of funds tied up by purchases or sales", "wages taking a percentage of the ratios of payments actually received to total sales", "awards on special contributions", "sharing out bonus according to both work performances and shares of capitals", and "fuzzy awards". In the Chuangda company, following reforms in ownership, all time-based wages that had been applied during the pre-reform period were abolished. The piece rate wage system was applied to those employees whose work performances are quantifiable; in addition, the yearly-salary system was applied to all office workers and top managers of all economically independent units. In addition, a system of "post-based wages" is applied to all supplementary staff and a system of "wages taking a percentage of profits" is applied to all marketing personnel.

In order to compare the structural changes of wages between Guangzheng and Chuangda, we classify all the items of wages into three groups – basic wage, bonus and subsidy. Our data on workers' earnings are as of December. 1997's earnings only include wages, while those for 2001 also include share bonuses.

First of all, the total earnings (wages) are not significantly different between Guangzheng and Chuangda in 1997, with Chuangda's being slightly higher than Guangzheng's. But, in 2001, although the total earnings had increased greatly in both companies, differences did exist: Guangzheng's average annual growth rate of earnings is 40 percentage points higher than Chuangda's from 1997 to 2001. What is more important, there were some structural changes. After ownership reforms, workers from both companies received share bonuses in addition to wages. Specifically, in Chuangda the proportion of the share bonuses to the total earnings was about 15 percent; while this proportion was much higher (near 25 percent) in Guangzheng. It is also worth noting that these two companies are different from each other in tersm of the structure of wages from 1997 to 2001. For example, in Guangzheng the proportions of basic wages and subsidies were reduced and that bonus as an instrument of incentives is introduced. From Table 4.2, we can find that Guangzheng's proportions of "basic wage" and "subsidy" are 5 and 10 percentage points lower than those of Chuangda, respectively.

Secondly, we compare the wages (earnings) between the two companies. In order to keep the consistence of the samples, we select 121 and 36 workers from Guangzheng and Chuangda companies, respectively.[3] In Figure 4.1, the workers selected are listed in an increasing order of wages (earnings). As for Guangzheng company, all of the workers with the lowest wages in December 1997 had received much higher wages and earnings (shown in left side of Figure 4.1a).

---

[3] Guangzheng's 121 workers are composed of 0.9% high-ranking staff, 5.3% middle-ranking staff, 2.6% office workers, 20.2% technical workers and 71.1% physical workers; of which female workers account for 50%. Chuangda's 36 workers are composed of 13.9% high-ranking staff, 50.0% middle-ranking staff, 27.8% office workers, and 8.3% physical workers; of which female workers account for 30.6%.

Table 4.2. Level, composition and inequality of earnings per worker, December

	Guangzheng			Chuangda		
	1997	2001		1997	2001	
		All staff	Excl. laid-off staff		All staff	Excl. laid-off staff
Total earnings (yuan)	490.64	723.39	735.54	493.97	528.20	660.63
(%)	(100.0)	(100.0)	(100.0)	(100.0)	(100.0)	(100.0)
Wages (yuan)	490.64	552.07	563.63	493.97	447.14	566.38
(%)	(100.0)	(76.3)	(76.6)	(100.0)	(84.7)	(85.7)
Share bonus	NA	171.32	171.91	NA	81.06	94.25
(%)		(23.7)	(23.4)		(15.3)	(14.3)
Of wages						
Basic wage (yuan)	340.36	376.60	384.48	354.90	260.86	330.42
(%)	(69.4)	(52.1)	(52.3)	(71.8)	(49.4)	(50.0)
Bonus (yuan)	NA	49.89	50.95	NA	NA	NA
(%)		(6.9)	(6.9)			
Subsidy (yuan)	150.28	125.58	128.20	139.07	186.28	235.96
(%)	(30.6)	(17.4)	(17.4)	(28.2)	(35.3)	(35.7)
Earnings inequalities (Gini coefficients)						
Total earnings	0.265	0.345	0.326	0.186	0.414	0.276
Wages	0.265	0.362	0.320	0.186	0.405	0.247
Share bonus	NA	0.595	0.601	NA	0.592	0.590
Of wages						
Basic wage	0.355	0.423	0.411	0.247	0.394	0.233
Subsidy	0.524	0.387	0.373	0.419	0.594	0.461
Samples	229	390	382	36	437	345

Notes: (1) monetary values are represented by current prices. From 1997 to 2001, the consumers price index (CPI) decreased by 2 percent (NBS, 2002, p. 296). (2) "NA" denotes not available. (3) The samples of Chuangda only come from office workers in 1997, which are not comparable to those in 2001.

However, the rest of the workers received different compensations in 2001 as compared the situation in 1997 (shown in the right side of Figure 4.1a). As for Chuangda company, all of the 36 workers were entitled to receive higher compensations in 2001 than in 1997 (see Figure 4.1b).

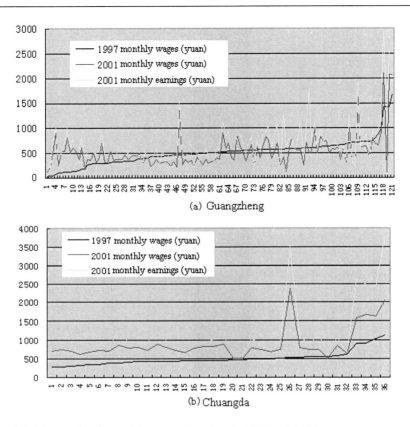

Figure 4.1. The workers' monthly wages (earnings), 1997 and 2001.

Thirdly, we also calculated the Gini coefficients of earnings (see Table 4.2) in order to measure the inequality index of earnings. A noticeable fact is that, following ownership reforms, the inequality of total earnings increased considerably. Between 1997 and 2001, Guangzheng's Gini coefficient of total earnings increased from 0.265 up to 0.326 (for samples excluding laid-off workers) or 0.345 (for all samples). Even though Chuangda's samples are not representative of its entire staff in 1997, its data do show great inequalities of earnings in 2001, with a Gini coefficient of 0.276 (for samples excluding laid-off workers) or 0.414 (for all samples). Obviously, the ownership reforms have led to an increasingly big gap of earnings between workers in each company.

The differences of production patterns and internal organizations between the two companies may influence, to a certain extent, the earnings gaps with each company. For example, Guangzheng was still able to reply on its coal production as a stable source of revenue, while Chuangda had to develop other new businesses since its coal resources were already exhausted in 1996. After losing its comparative advantages in coal production, Chuangda faced more challenges than Guangzheng during the period of ownership reforms.

Finally, the Gini coefficients of the share bonus (about 0.60) are much higher than those of the wages in both companies. This indicates that a small portion of staff in both companies secured most of the share bonuses. We can thus conclude that the unequal distribution of share bonuses is the major source for the increasing gaps of earnings. Taking Chuangda as an example: the unequal distribution of share bonuses enlarged the Gini coefficient of total earnings by 2.2 percent (for all samples) or 11.7 percent (for samples excluding laid-off workers). On the other hand, the laid-off workers also resulted in the increasing inequalities of earnings. According to our estimates, affected by laid-off workers, between 1997 and 2001 Guangzheng's Gini coefficients of total earnings and of wages rose by 6 percent and 13 percent, respectively. This influence was more obviously in Chuangda. From 1997 to 2001, Chuangda's Gini coefficients of total earnings and of wages increased by 50 percent and 64 percent, respectively.

4.4. THE DETERMINANTS OF EARNINGS WITHIN FIRMS

Past empirical studies have demonstrated that human capital is the most important factor in the determinants of compensations of labors. Human capital, embodied in each laborer, is composed of knowledge, skills as well as other capabilities cohered in the body of each laborer. According to Schulz (1961), these capabilities are the major factor contributing to the growth of production. Economic growth replies on the quality of human capital not on the abundance of natural resources. The empirical studies on the earnings of labors show that, along with the process of marketization of the Chinese economy, human capital's influences on earnings have increased (Li and Li, 1993; Knight and Song, 1993; Lai, 1999; and Gustafsson and Li, 2001). According to Gustafsson and Li (2000), gender's gaps of earning rose in urban China during the 1990s. It is more noticeable that the increased share of the earnings gaps have stemmed from the society's prejudices and discriminations against women.

Table 4.3 shows that workers with higher levels of education also had a more rapid growth in earnings. For example, in 2001 Guangzheng's average earnings of workers graduated from colleges and senior high schools are 2.65 and 1.86 times those in 1997, respectively. Chuangda's average earnings of workers graduated from colleges and senior high schools in 2001 are 2.13 and 1.11 times those in 1997, respectively.

Table 4.3. Average earnings by groups of workers (yuan/person, December)

| | | 1997 | | 2001 | | | |
| | | Wages | | Wages | | Total earnings | |
		Guangzheng	Chuangda	Guangzheng	Chuangda	Guangzheng	Chuangda
All staff		490.64	493.07	552.07	447.14	723.39	528.20
Sex	Male	582.46	533.42	709.67	475.11	933.65	576.55
	Female	435.93	404.29	358.03	390.76	501.26	437.13
Education	College (3 and 4 years)	509.46	562.69	1163.06	857.61	1348.53	1198.52
	Senior high or technical school	493.76	442.17	671.03	402.36	916.99	492.77
	Junior high school	513.45	530.89	469.07	415.19	637.66	460.38
	Primary	484.90	–	533.42	733.65	740.60	787.82
	Others	467.75	–	498.05	505.04	560.71	506.25
Age group	20 year or younger	–	277.90	426.27	–	426.27	24.17
	21–30 years	494.85	339.28	584.80	345.76	679.72	389.63
	31–40 years	493.48	512.43	511.22	485.55	665.72	582.45
	41–50 years	614.23	560.30	660.64	465.48	1018.20	549.90
	50 years or older	–	–	572.72	356.36	688.50	429.91
Position	Physical workers	477.66	515.52	438.46	515.38	581.00	563.99
	Technical workers	515.10	–	534.25	433.80	699.17	482.88
	Office workers	312.38	348.21	777.17	640.24	1036.71	703.18
	Middle-rank staff	1066.96	457.90	1742.14	754.04	2910.69	1056.02
	High-rank staff	1416.65	885.02	2281.74	1654.73	2575.06	2721.39

From the perspective of positions, the average earnings of three groups of high- and middle-rank staff and office workers changed more quickly than those of the other workers. For example, in Guangzheng these three groups' average earnings in 2001 were 1.82, 2.72 and 3.32 times those in 1997, respectively; while they were 3.07, 2.31 and 2.02 times those in Chuangda, respectively. It must be noted that the different levels of earnings among various groups of workers, shown in Table 4.3, do not sufficiently reflect the influences of these group variables (such as age, sex, education and position). In fact, some group variables are related to each other. For example, many high-rank managers usually hold high levels of education; while physical workers are often young; etc.

In order to estimate how these explanatory variables have individually contributed to the changes of earnings, let us apply a simple model that has been widely used by labor economists:

$$\ln(\text{Wage})=\beta_0+\beta_1\text{Experience}+\beta_2\text{Experience}^2+\beta_3\text{Male}+\beta_4\text{Education}+\beta_5\text{Position}$$

In the above model, $\ln(\text{Wage})$, the dependent variable, is the natural log of wages.[4] "Experience" and "Experience^2" denote the length of work experience (in working years) and its square. "Male" denotes male workers; and "Education" is represented by the length of education in years (its data are calculated based on *Zichuan Annuals 1990*). "Position" includes four dummies: "high-rank staff", "middle-rank staff", "office workers" and "technical workers". "Physical workers" are treated as a comparison variable and, thus, excluded from regressions.

From the estimated results (shown in Table 4.4a), we may find that some explanatory variables are playing differing roles in the determinants of wages from 1997 to 2001. In 1997, for example, the estimated coefficient on "Education" is not statistically significant, indicating that education background was not taken into account in the determination of wages within Guangzheng. Might education variable exert an influence on wages through various position variables? However, our estimated results do not support this hypothesis.

Since the estimated coefficients on "Office workers" and "Technical workers" are negative, indicating that, in 1997 the average level of monthly wages of office and technical workers was, ceteris paribus, lower than that of physical workers in Guangzheng.

In addition, "Experience", also a factor contributing to human capitals and, of course, to the level of a worker's earnings under a market-oriented system, only had a negative coefficient in 1997. That is to say, a worker's level of wages is negatively related to his or her work experience (represented by working years) at the beginning of employment in Guangzheng. The coefficient on "Male", which is positive, is only statistically insignificant, showing that gender discrimination did not exist in the determination of wages in 1997.

---

[4] Since "share bonus" has nothing to do with workers' performances, we will not test the regression in which the dependent variable is represented by either "share bonus" or "total earning".

Table 4.4a. Determinants of wages, Guangzheng, 1997 and 2001

	1997				2001			
	Education as dummies		Education as a continuous variable		Education as dummies		Education as a continuous variable	
	Coefficient	T- statistic	Coefficient	T- statistic	Coefficient	T- statistic	Coefficient	T- statistic
Constant	6.819	20.091^a	6.820	13.926^a	5.944	49.95^a	5.503	24.95^a
Experience	-0.146	-2.961^a	-0.116	-2.521^a	0.0172	1.27^c	0.015	1.08
Experience^2	0.0051	2.961^a	0.0037	2.393^a	-0.0002	-0.46	0.00001	0.03
Male	0.163	1.198	0.138	1.002	0.314	5.52^a	0.303	5.27^a
Education	-	-	-0.022	-0.474	-	-	0.0536	3.06^a
High-rank staff	0.772	1.153	1.051	1.585^c	1.114	5.30^a	1.151	5.44^a
Middle-rank staff	0.813	2.586^a	0.747	2.343^a	1.144	8.02^a	1.091	7.75^a
Office workers	-1.081	-2.441^a	-1.184	-2.820^a	-0.011	-0.08	-0.015	-0.12
Technical workers	-	-	-0.135	-0.865	-0.004	-0.06	-0.013	-0.19
Physical workers	0.113	0.732	-	-	-	-	-	-
College	-0.394	-1.113	-	-	0.466	3.89^a	-	-
Senior-high school	-0.194	-1.323^c	-	-	0.024	0.37	-	-
Junior high school	-	-	-	-	-	-	-	-
Primary school	-0.788	-1.712^c	-	-	0.021	0.14	-	-
R^2	0.216		0.186		0.396		0.389	
F	3.176		3.335		22.2		26.55	
Samples	125		125		324		322	

Notes: (1) Based on ordinary least squares (OLS) regressions, with the natural log of monthly wages as the dependent variable. (2) '-' denotes explanatory variables are excluded from the regressions. ^{a} and ^{c} denote statistically significant at the 1% and 10% levels, respectively.

Table 4.4b. Determinants of wages, Chuangda, 2001

	2001			
	Education as dummies		Education as a continuous variable	
	Coefficient	T- statistic	Coefficient	T- statistic
Constant	5.860	33.87[a]	5.898	18.99[a]
Experience	0.030	1.84[c]	0.030	1.81[c]
Experience^2	-0.0008	-2.16[a]	-0.0009	-2.19[a]
Male	0.169	2.56[a]	0.177	2.71[a]
Education	-	-	-0.0075	-0.30
High-rank staff	1.133	4.91[a]	1.195	5.25[a]
Middle-rank staff	0.451	3.77[a]	0.449	3.64[a]
Office workers	0.421	3.22[a]	0.396	3.04[a]
Technical workers	-0.193	-1.51[c]	-0.229	-1.79[c]
Physical workers	-	-	-	-
College	0.010	0.070	-	-
Senior-high school	-0.093	-1.25[c]	-	-
Junior high school	-	-	-	-
Primary school	-0.387	1.13	-	-
R^2	0.231		0.223	
F	9.74		11.67	
Samples	334		334	

Notes: (1) Based on ordinary least squares (OLS) regressions, with the natural log of monthly wages as the dependent variable. (2) '-' denotes explanatory variables are excluded from the regressions. [a] and [c] denote statistically significant at the 1% and 10% levels, respectively. There is no regression for Chuangda in 1997 since the samples are not representative of Chuangda's whole staff.

Different from the 1997's estimated results, Guangzheng's "Experience", "Experience^2" are insignificantly estimated in 2001, suggesting that, after ownership reform, the level of wages was no longer related to work experience in Guangzheng. This may also indicate that the influences of work experience on labor productivity in traditional, labor-intensive industries are much less than that in other, especially capital-intensive, industries. The estimated coefficient on "Education" (i.e., 0.0536), which is statistically significant, is quite large, especially given that some position variables included in the regression also have positive effects on wages. Note that education's influences on workers' earnings may be partially included in the coefficients on position variables. In other words, if the position variables are not taken into account, the estimated coefficient on "Education" would rise accordingly. Obviously, Guangzheng's coefficient on education is even larger than those estimated in other empirical studies, all of the latter have omitted position variables in the regressions.[1]

The estimated results also show that the coefficients on the high- and middle-rank staff in 2001 are not only larger than those on office and technical workers, they are also larger than those in 1997. We can thus conclude that, as a result of ownership reform, high-rank staff received higher level of wages. At last, the estimated coefficient on "Male" is 0.303 (which is statistically significant at the 1 percent level), showing that, *ceteris paribus*, male workers' wages were 35.4 percent higher than female workers in 2001. It seems very likely that ownership reform might have resulted in some kind of gender discrimination in Guangzheng.

Compared with those of Guangzheng, Chuangda's estimated results have several differences in 2001 (see Table 4.4b). First, its coefficient on "Education" is not statistically significant, indicating that educational background was not emphasized in the determination of wages. Secondly, the estimated coefficient on other explanatory variables are different from those of Guangzheng. For example, the coefficient on "Experience" is positive and statistically significant, with a ratio of return to work experience (in years) of about 3 percent. Although gender difference existed in Chuangda, it is much less than that in Guangzheng in 2001. In addition, the gaps of wages between high- and middle-rank staff and the technical and physical workers in Chuangda are smaller than those in Guangzheng.

The two cases demonstrated in this section cannot be used to reach a general conclusion; neither can they illustrate the tales of other Chinese SOEs with similar experiences of transitions. But they do show that ownership reform has significantly influenced the distributional patterns of earnings in the two formerly state-owned, now shareholding, enterprises.

---

[1] For example, the estimated ratios of return to education are for 0.038 for urban China and 0.020 for rural China in 1988 (Li and Li, 1994, p. 445) and 0.042 for SOEs, and 0.032 for collectively-owned enterprises and 0.0791 for foreign-invested enterprises in 1996 (Zhao, 2001), and 0.044 for a large state-owned coal mine in 2000 (Guo, 2009, pp. 59-65).

Chapter 5

CHINA'S INTERPROVINCIAL DISPUTES AT LAKE WEISHAN

5.1. INTERPROVINCIAL RELATIONS AND LAKE WEISHAN

5.1.1. Interprovincial Relations in China

Most of China's provinces, autonomous regions and municipalities directly under the central government (in what follows, unless stated otherwise, we will use the term 'province' to denote all the three kinds of administrative divisions), which are the average size and scale of a European country in population and land area, are considerable political and economic systems in their own right. The differences between these provinces have long been a defining characteristic of China's politics since in most instances their boundaries have been created more than two thousand years ago (Gottmann, 1973; Goodman, 1997). China is one of the countries with the most complicated topography and diversified physical environment in the world. Furthermore, China's provinces are not homogeneous, in terms of ethnic and linguistic groups as well as provincial politics. As a result, the chances of the adoption of a common standard and interprovincial coordination between different groups of people are not likely to be enhanced if there are markedly differing religious beliefs and cultural values.

Glancing at the map of China, one may find that many administrative regions, especially provinces, have natural geographical barriers such as mountains, rivers, lakes, and so on. This kind of geographical separation between adjacent provinces could have a serious effect on regional economic development if the interprovincial transport and communication linkages are established inefficiently. After checking the highway networks of ten provinces (Beijing, Shanghai,

Tianjin, Hebei, Shanxi, Liaoning, Gansu, Qinghai, Inner Mongolia and Ningxia) in *China Atlas* published in 1983, for example, Guo (1993, p. 119) estimates that, of the 453 highways in the peripheral areas, around 60 percent were transprovincially connected, whereas about 40 percent did not reach their respective province's border. Obviously, the fragmentary nature of the highway networks has exacerbated the inconveniences for every sphere of the local inhabitant's lives and have had a particularly adverse effect on the Chinese economy.[1]

Many provinces, autonomous regions and municipalities directly under the central government have been informally demarcated in China. As a result, cross-border relations between the relevant provinces have never been easily coordinated and, sometimes, could become a destabilizing source for social stability and economic development. After 1986, the Ministry of Civil Affairs (MCA) conducted a series of field surveys on the provinces of Xinjiang, Inner Mongolia, Ningxia, Gansu, Shaanxi, Qinghai, Jilin, Hebei and Shandong in order to provide legal, formal, geographical boundaries for those provinces. Many problems, however, still remained unsolved. For example, after having compared the locally mapped borders, Zhang (1990, p. 8) points out that among China's 66 cross-province border lines (about 52,000 km), 59 cross-province borders have been discordantly portrayed and 54 cross-province borders have been disputed by the relevant local governments along a section of about 9,500 km long borders.

Moreover, there is another geographical characteristic in the Chinese economy: many provinces' borders are naturally marked by mountains, rivers and lakes which bless the border regions with abundant natural and environmental resources. Given the cross-border *imbroglios* between the provinces, the sustainable exploitation and utilization of natural resources (such as energy, metals, forests, fishery and so on) as well as environmental protection in the border regions will undoubtedly pose problems and disputes for both central and local governments in China. Non-cooperative cross-border relations between provinces could eventually become a source of disturbance to economic development. Even worse, some interprovincial disputes led to armed conflicts and seriously affected the social security and economic sustainability in border regions regardless of the regulations concerning the resolution of border disputes between administrative regions issued by the State Council (1988).

For example, of China's 66 interprovincial borderlines, 65 are disputed and have even been published, according to their own preferences, by the provincial-

---

[1] Examples of literature would include *Economic News* (1987, p. 1; 1988, p. 1), Hu (1992, p. 1), and Guo (1993, pp. 118–23; 1996, pp. 70–1).

level authorities in their official maps and documents (Zhang, 1990, p. 8). According to the statistics released by the Ministry of Civil Affairs, of the 52,000 km of interprovincial borders in the People's Republic of China, only 5 percent are legally fixed; 77 percent are regarded as informal (or customary borderlines); and about 18 percent (about 9,500 km) remain the subject of active disputes.[2] According to the various sources, there were more than 800 cases of cross-border disputes in 333 of the 849 interprovincial border counties of almost all provinces. The total disputed areas (about 140,000 km^2) include grassland (about 96,000 km^2), mining areas (about 5000 km^2), water (about 1000 km^2) and mixed grass-mining-forestland (about 30,000 km^2) and are distributed unevenly in the Western belt (about 130,000 km^2), the Central belt (about 17,000 km^2) and the Eastern belt (about 700 km^2).[3] In defiance of the State Council (1988) regulations concerning the resolution of interprovincial border disputes, many disputes were the subject of armed fights between different groups of people. This has seriously affected the social security and sustainability of economic development in those cross-border areas.

5.1.2. Focus on Lake Weishan

This chapter is based on two field surveys on Lake Weishan conducted in 2000 and 2002, respectively.[4] During the era of the People's Republic of China, from 1949 to the early 21st century, the interprovincial tensions at Lake Weishan have been aggravated by the ambiguity in the interprovincial delimitation, a lack of respect for the rule of law on interprovincial relations, and both central and provincial government nepotism. The establishment of a new province surrounding the Lake Weishan area is presented as a possible solution to the interprovincial border disputes as well as a means for improving the administrative efficiency in this marginalized area.

---

[2] See *Beijing Youth*, 2 December 2002 (available at www.sina.com.cn).
[3] See *Baokan Wenzhai* (1989, p. 4).
[4] Professor Hu Xuwei of Institute of Geographical Science and Natural Resources, The Chinese Academy of Sciences (CAS), joined the first visit to the whole border area of Jiangsu and Shandong provinces. Thanks are due to officials of Weishan county (Shandong province) and Peixian county (Jiangsu province), who not only told us stories about the Lake Weishan disputes but also gave us generous help for our stay at Lake Weishan. I am grateful to Dr. Zhao Jun (Xuzhou Municipal Government, Jiangsu province) for arranging our field investigation and Mr. Yu Haijian (Economic and Trade Commission of Shandong Province) for providing data on Lake Weishan. I also gratefully acknowledge Dr. David Lawrence (Resource Management in Asia-Pacific (RMAP) Program in the Australian National University) who helped me in correcting many parts of the chapter and Mr. Guo Liqing for his superb research assistance.

Lake Weishan is located on the border of Shandong and Jiangsu provinces in East China mid-way between Shanghai and Beijing (see Figure 1). It is composed of four connected sub-lakes – Dushan, Nanyang, Zhaoyang, and Weishan, and is also identified by an alternative name, Nansihu (four southern lakes). However, the name Weishan is preferred here. As the largest fresh water reservoir (with an area of 1260 square kilometers) in northern China, Lake Weishan receives water from 53 rivers in a broad catchment area spread across 32 counties and cities of four provinces (Jiangsu, Shandong, Henan and Anhui). The maximum capacity of the lake is 4.73 billion cubic meters (SBWC, 2002, p. 1).

For centuries Lake Weishan has been an important storage area of fresh water, but it also assists in the prevention of flooding, the production of aquatic products, as the route of local shipping, and the source of water for agricultural and industrial production. It remains vital to the daily life of the residents of 14 cities and counties (districts) in Jiangsu and Shandong provinces. In addition, Lake Weishan contains 79 species of fish, 74 types of water-related plants, 364 plankton species and 87 identified species of bird. The local saying is Lake Weishan is capable of "producing ten litres of gold per day" (ri chu doujin).[5] High-quality coal resources have also been discovered beneath the lake. These are seen as extremely important by the economic policy-makers at both central and provincial level government in China.

Lake Weishan was an important area in ancient China. According to archaeologists, the cultural relics and objects discovered in the region are evidence of early human activity dating from as early as five or six thousand years ago.[6] During the Song (960–1279 AD), the Yuan (1279–1368 AD), the Ming (1368–1644 AD) and the Qing (1644–1911 AD) dynasties, Lake Weishan was shared by two provinces and seven counties (the current Yutai, Jining, Zoucheng, Tengzhou and Yicheng counties of Shandong province in the North and Southeast; and Peixian and Tongshan counties of Jiangsu province in the West and Southwest). During the period of the War of Resistance Against the Japanese Troops (1937–45) it was a region of armed resistance against Japanese occupation. A Squadron of Volunteer Army (kangri yiyong zongdui) was established in the lake area. This squadron included the No. 1 Group of No. 1 Detachment, South Shandong Railroad Force (the Railroad Guerrillas), the [Beijing–Hangzhou] Grand Canal Detachment, and the Lake Military Group.

In July 1944, the border county of Peixian–Tengzhou (then known as Pei–Teng Bianxian) was renamed Lincheng county, while the latter was composed of

---

[5] Cited from CCPCWC and PGWC (1998).
[6] In what follows in this section, unless stated otherwise, all data are cited from *Weishan County Annuals* (2000).

nine districts, with a prefectural office located in Xiazhen township. In October 1944, the western parts of Zoucheng and Tenzhou counties were merged to form Fushan county, which was composed of today's Fushan county in the North and the border areas of the present day Peixian, Tongshan and Lincheng counties in the South. When the People's Republic of China was founded, Weishan county was cut into eight counties under separate administration from Shandong and Jiangsu provinces. In September 1949, a Working Committee of the Chinese Communist Party was established with an Administrative Office at the lake area. This working committee had jurisdiction over northern Xuzhou municipality and the four lakes areas of Weishan, Zhaoyang, Dushan and Nanyang as well as villages with proximity to those lakes.

Prior to 1953, most of Lake Weishan was part of Xuzhou Administrative Region, and under the jurisdiction of Shandong province. 90 percent of the southern part of Lake Weishan was shared by two counties (Peixian and Tongshan); and the eastern part of the lake was part of the Seventh District of Peixian county, with Xiazhen township being the administrative center of the District. This district comprised eight towns and more than 100 villages.

In 1953, Xuzhou Administrative Region was transferred from Shandong to Jiangsu province. During the process of territorial re-adjustment, Shandong province submitted a proposal that, for sake of the unified administration and the public security of the entire lake area, the sub-lakes of Zhaoyang and Weishan, together with some villages of Tongshan county (all of which had been under the jurisdiction of Jiangsu province), should comprise a new county (Weishan) and be placed under the administration of Shandong province. This proposal was submitted to the Ministry of Civil Affairs (MCA) by the Administrative Commission of East China Region on 17 July 1953 (dongbanzi [53] official letter, No. 0643) and supported by the People's Government of Shandong province on 4 May 1953 (luminzi [53] official letter, No. 1533).

The interprovincial border set at that time followed principles set by the Central Government: Shandong's Weishan county was to be separated from Jiangsu's Peixian and Tongshan counties by the border between the lake's waterline and lakeside land, with the exception of a few of villages located outside the lakeside land. These villages were set as border markers between the two provinces. The State Administrative Council, the former State Council, approved this proposal on 22 August 1953 (zhengzhengbuzi [53] official letter, No. 136). The newly established county of Weishan was entitled to administer 267 villages and four towns.[7] In March 1956, the counties of Fushan and Xuecheng were also put under Weishan's administration. However, from May to September of the same year, some villages were transferred from Weishan county to Xuzhou municipality of Jiangsu province and others were transferred from Yixian, Jiaxiang and Jining counties of Shandong province to Weishan county. In early 1984, another 14 villages from Peixian county in Jiangsu province were transferred to Weishan county in Shandong province.

As a result of the above administrative re-adjustments, the county of Weishan now contains 565 administrative villages and five neighborhood committees, covering a total geographical area of 1780 square kilometers (this includes 514 square kilometers of lake). As of 2001, Weishan county had a total population of 682,000. The majority are Han Chinese but 25 other ethnic minorities, including Muslim, Miao, Mongol, Zhuang, Manchu, Korean, Yi, and Hani, are also resident in Weishan.[8]

5.2. THE BOUNDARY DISPUTES AT LAKE WEISHAN

5.2.1. Reasons for Discord

During the 20th century, the Lake Weishan area has experienced drastic changes in provincial administration. This has placed the Shandong–Jiangsu interprovincial relation on an unstable foundation. The 1953 border readjustment scheme created many problems. The fact that changes in natural conditions could result in either a rise (during the rainy season) or a fall (during the dry season) of the water level in Lake Weishan, which would in turn either reduce or increase the size of lake and lakeshore land, was not taken into consideration. Naturally, this would cause frequent changes in the location of the interprovincial borderline which followed the decision that: "Wherever water reaches is under Shandong's jurisdiction; but the land is regarded as Jiangsu's territory."

In addition, it was clearly assumed in the 1953 border delimitation scheme that the whole area of the lake should be under the exclusive administration of Weishan county in Shandong province. Jiangsu residents living along the lakeside were permitted to continue conducting their lake-related businesses, such as fishing in the lake and farming in the lakeside land.

---

[7] Source: The State Administrative Council of the PRC (under the form of Letter zhengzhengbuzi, No. 136), 22 August 1953. According to the *Weishan Statistical Yearbook 2001* (p. 1), the total number of villages was 302.

[8] Source: *Weishan Statistical Yearbook 2001*, p. 2.

During the first years, when Shandong province exercised its governance over the whole area, Jiangsu province did not fully realize the lake's crucial importance to the agricultural and industrial economy of the region, nor was there sufficient recognition of the area's importance to the people's livelihood. It was only when Jiangsu province attempted to build an iron-ore mine in Liguo at the southern side of Lake Weishan, in an area near the provincial borders, that debate strengthened. The mining proposal was impeded in 1956 and this stimulated the Jiangsu administrators to demand the return of 35 villages which had been transferred to Shandong province in 1953.

The central government in Beijing agreed to Jiangsu's request in principle but still kept the whole lake under the sole administration of Weishan county (OLL, 1996). Since that time Jiangsu has increasingly sought to gain strategic recognition of the lake as part of its provincial economy. In 1958, Shandong province decided to construct a dam, which effectively divided the whole lake into two parts – an upper lake and a lower lake (see Figure 5.1).

While the construction of the dam in the middle of the lake was good for the provincial economy of Shandong province it was not beneficial to the economy of Jiangsu province. Jiangsu had no administrative jurisdiction over Lake Weishan, and could neither change Shandong's construction scheme nor exercise any control over water rights. Not only did the dam result in 90 percent of the lake's water reserves being contained on the Shandong side of the border, but it also submerged 210,000 mu [one mu is approximately equal to 667 square meters] of arable land on the Jiangsu side. Even worse, it made the farmers of Peixian district completely unable to irrigate their crops during a drought or to drain their waterlogged fields after heavy rain (OLL, 1996).

The central government made great efforts to resolve the Lake Weishan disputes and these attempts can be traced through three documents issued by the Chinese Communist Party Central Committee and the State Council in 1984 (This will be further discussed in Section 5.3). The three documents, which transferred disputed areas and villages from Jiangsu to Shandong, provide a large part of the present administrative picture of the Shandong–Jiangsu border area issues (see Figure 5.2(a)).

However, the Shandong and Jiangsu provincial governments have each chosen to interpret the three central documents in a different manner. The result has been uncertainty over the interprovincial border and a lack of resolution of what is a fundamental border demarcation issue.

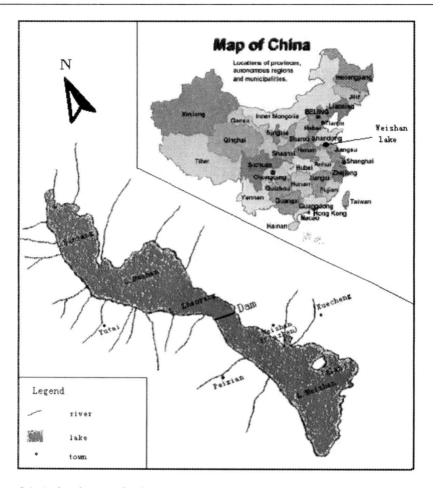

Figure 5.1. A sketch map of Lake Weishan.

Over the course of the following years, the Shandong administrators emphasized an exact implementation of the three central documents, insisting that Lake Weishan should be under the sole administration of Weishan county. However, the Jiangsu administrators argued that the decisions made by the central government were unfair (WOLA, 1998). Jiangsu suggested that the use of the widely recognized principle on water-area delimitation that "shared lakes are divided along the deepest line") (see Figures 2(b)). Both provinces had far too many differences to reach an agreement.[9]

---

[9] Based on the author's two talks with officials in Weishan and Peixian counties on 1 and 2 June 2000, respectively.

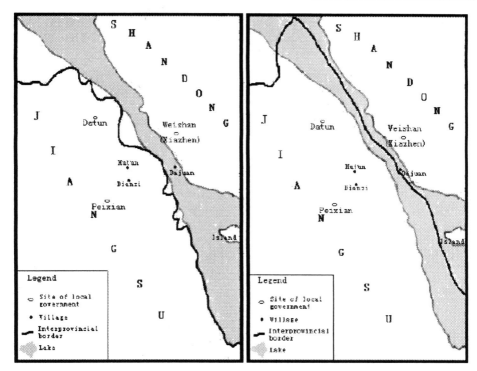

(a) Based on the map of administrative division of Weishan county (drawn by the government of Weishan county, published by Xi'an Map Press, Xi'an, Shaanxi province, 1995.

(b) Based on the map of administrative division of Peixian county (drawn by the Surveying and Drawing Academy of Xuzhou Municipality, edited by the government of Peixian county, published by China Map Press, Beijing, 1995.

Figure 5.2. The differently defined borders between Shandong and Jiangsu provinces.

5.2.2. Consequences

The argument about the ownership of Lake Weishan continued, as did the border conflict between the provinces. Between the founding of the People's Republic of China in 1949 and the year 2000 there have been nearly 400 cases of cross-border conflicts in the region, with nearly 400 people killed or seriously wounded. The details are: 16 people died and 24 people were disabled in Peixian county; four people died in Weishan county; as well as numerous casualties in Tongshan and Fengxian counties of Jiangsu province (WOLA, 1998). The main causes for these causalities came from fights between the cultivators of the lakeside land and fishermen operating other lake-related business, as well as workers involved in the construction of various water conservancy, public security, construction of communication equipment programs and the collectors of fees and taxes for use of lake related resources.

The Shandong–Jiangsu border disputes have seriously affected the social solidarity and public security of the Lake Weishan area. In addition, due to the lack of appropriate coordination between all stakeholders concerned, natural and environmental resources have been overexploited or destroyed. The border disputes have damaged the ecological sustainability of the lake and caused a substantial amount of environmental degradation. Since the 1990s, along with the rapid development of industrial enterprises in the area, industrial wastes and pollutants had been discharged directly via 53 rivers that all feed into the lake, at the rate of over 570,000 tons per day (see Table 5.2). From 1992 to 1998, there had been 23 major pollution accidents, resulting in a direct loss to the local economy of 80 million yuan (CCPCWC and PGWC, 1998).

During our field inspections, we found that five major rivers, the Chengguo, Xiaoni, Peiyan, Zhengji and the Sulu, have been the major polluting sources. Freshwater fish and important limnobiological plants were no longer present around the mouths of these rivers. There are generally more than ten pollution accidents in the lake per year. On the eve of the Spring Festival (the traditional Chinese new year holiday) in January 1988, a pollution accident occurred in the southern coast of Lake Weishan that left more than 400,000 residents in the northern district of Xuzhou city with no fresh water supply. 18 factories had to stop production for 20 days.[10]

Water pollution has not only endangered the local fishery and the collection of limnological plants, but it has also affected the daily lives and health of the nearby residents. According to a survey conducted by a correspondent of Qilu Evening News, the frequency of cancer causing illnesses and tumors has been much higher in the lake region than in the nearby inland areas. Reported health events related to liver diseases, diarrhoea and birth defects have also been much more frequent in the polluted area than in the non-polluted area.

For example the following case was reported in the *Qilu Evening News* (1997):

> "Located at the mouth of Chengguo River, Shadi village, Liuzhuang township in Weishan county, has a population of 1000 persons and an area of over 20,000 mu of shoaly land. Due to the lack of arable land (with a per capita

---

[10] Source: Released by officials in charge of economic planning and environmental protection of Xuzhou municipal government in a meeting sponsored by the author at Nanjiao Hotel, Xuzhou city, Jiangsu province, 24 May 2000.

area of only 0.013 mu), most of the residents were used to taking reeds, lotus-roots and other lake-related resources. Fishing and fishery cultivation has been their major sources of living. During recent years, as industrial and living waste water discharged from Tengzhou city into Lake Weishan via Chengguo River has increased, water sources on which the residents have depended for their living have been seriously polluted. Consequently, fish stocks have been extinguished, and limnological plants have died. Even worse, the health conditions of the residents living in the region have been seriously affected. Since 1988, 26 young residents have died from diseases caused by, as diagnosed by hospitals at county or higher levels, the drinking of the polluted well water."

Table 5.1. Casualties in selected armed fights at Lake Weishan, 1961–98

No.	MM/DD/Year	Weapons used	Deaths	Wounded
1	11/18/1961	Duck gun, javelin, sword, stick, etc.	1	2
2	10/12/1971	Duck gun, reaphook	1	>10
3	10/15/1973	Duck gun, self-made gun	4	55
4	10/11/1980	Self-made gun, reaping hook, bayonet, shovel, scourge, spear, dagger, etc	3	35
5	10/19/1980	Rifle, light machine gun	1	47
6	9/13/1983	Rifle	3	1
7	10/22/1986	Rifle	1	7
8	6/5/1990	Dynamite, rifle, cannons, grenade, lance, stick	3	11
9	2/17/1995	Police pistol	1	-
10	5/17/1998	NA	1	-

Sources: (1) Office of Lakeside Land, Peixian county, Jiangsu province; and (2) Magistrate Office of Weishan county, Shandong province.

Table 5.2. Water pollution at Lake Weishan, 1995–2000 (unit: mg/l)

Year	TOTP (Total phosphate)	COD (Chemical oxygen demand)
1995	0.08	8.01
1996	0.20	6.16
1997	0.18	8.43
1998	0.19	11.64
1999	0.18	9.64
2000	0.15	8.05

Note: In China, standards for polluted water are defined as: TOTP>0.09 mg/l and COD>6mg/l.
Source: Bureau of Environmental Protection, Shandong province, October 2002.

5.3. How Have the Disputes Been Resolved?

Since the interprovincial border of Lake Weishan was not accurately marked
by the central government in 1953, the handover of the lakeside land from
Tongshan county to Weishan county was not formally implemented. Peixian
county only transferred 15 villages and the related population and land to Weishan
county. The Jiangsu's residents in Peixian and Tongshan counties continued their
farming and other lake-related businesses in the lakeside lands and waters. The
situation appeared to be settled during the first years following the establishment
of Weishan county but, in 1959, Weishan county complained that Peixian had
cultivated 80,000mu of land for wheat without authorization along the lakeside.
Subsequently, in 1960, Weishan county re-distributed all the lakeside land that
had been publicly or privately owned by the Jiangsu side to farmers or companies
of Shandong province. Since then, interprovincial relations have worsened (OLL,
1998).

As described earlier, the size and scope of the lakeside land changes
frequently due to natural conditions. Therefore, whenever disputes occurred, it
was usually very difficult to find an effective solution. This can be witnessed by
the two consultative meetings on the resolution of border conflicts held between
15 August and 15 December 1961, by Jiangsu and Shandong provinces first in
Xuzhou and then in Ji'nan. During the consultations, Shandong insisted that:

(1) the interprovincial border should be defined on the basis of the document
     approved by the State Administrative Council in 1953;
(2) all the lands within Shandong's border, regardless of whether they were
     owned by Jiangsu, should be returned to Weishan county; and
(3) the lake-related resources, regardless of who owned or operated them,
     should be returned to Weishan, if they were covered by lake water. In
     addition, Weishan county suggested that, for the sake of promoting
     production and avoiding further conflicts, all villages within five
     kilometers of the lake should be transferred to Shandong province.[11]

Since the central government was not involved in this consultation, the three-
month interprovincial meeting did not result in any agreements of any substance.

Usually, armed disputes in the Lake Weishan were resolved by the relevant
local authorities. However, there have been a few extremely serious examples.
These have been resolved by higher-level authorities from both sides concerned. It

---

[11] Cited from OLL (1961).

was told that the self-resolved cases have not been documented[12] but that from the 1960s to the mid-1980s, there were six jointly-resolved cases for the armed fights in 1961, 1967, 1973, 1980, 1981, and 1984. The resolution of the conflicts required participation by officials from both provinces and the related counties. However, since most resolutions were not mediated by the central government, they did not resolve the fundamental problems underlying the disputes. Each side, Shandong and Jiangsu, only emphasized their own interests. Only some minor border-related problems were resolved.

Some of the resolution processes are useful case studies.

5.3.1. The Nanjing Accord

During the wheat-harvesting season in 1967, the Production Command Department (shengchan zhihui bu) of the Revolutionary Committee of Shandong province (the de facto provincial-level government organ in Shandong at that period) reported to the State Council that farmers from Peixian and Tongshan counties of Jiangsu province were conducting agricultural activities beyond their provincial border. Zhou En'lai, then Premier of the State Council, appointed General Du Ping, the Commissar of Nanjing Military District (NMD) of the Central Military Committee of the Chinese Communist Party, to convene a consultative meeting of leaders from the relevant cities and counties of Jiangsu and Shandong provinces and military representatives in Nanjing. Later, they came to reach an accord. This agreement, known as the Nanjing accord, stated that the lake-related products, while they could still be operated by Peixian county, should be under the sole administration of Weishan county. It also determined that "The arable land with a height of more than 32.5m (that is, from the mouth of the abrogated Yellow River) shall be jointly cultivated by all adjacent counties; while those with a height of less than 32.5m shall be cultivated by Weishan county alone, with the exception of a few lakeside land that still can be cultivated by farmers of Tongshan and Peixian counties."[13] With regard to the ownership of the lake-related resources, the accord only gave an in-principle agreement that "Those who have cultivated land shall own it." Besides, it re-emphasized that Weishan county was exclusively authoritative to administer all lake-related resources, to issue operation permission certificates, and to levy resource use taxes and fees.[14]

---

[12] Based on the author's talks with county officials in Peixian township, Jiangsu province on 2 June 2000.
[13] Cited from OLL (1998).
[14] Ibid.

Later on, the Nanjing accord was jointly issued by the State Council and the CCP's Central Military Committee in its No. [67]173 Ordinance.

Unfortunately, the Cultural Revolution of the late 1960s seriously impacted on the implementation of the Nanjing accord. Neither the accord nor the central ordinance was in force at that time. As a result the social and political environment around the lake was tense. To prevent possible conflicts, leaders from the two provinces met in Ji'nan city, the provincial capital of Shandong, to establish a united working group. This group commenced formal operations on 15 October 1973. The first task was the resolution of reed-harvesting conflicts. The second task was to seek ways in which a fundamental resolution of the cross-border disputes could be achieved. In the meantime, an armed fight between Dajuan brigade from Weishan county and Dianzi brigade from Peixian county broke out in which four brigade members were killed and 55 others were wounded (see Table 5.1).

After both sides finally reached a temporary agreement concerning the cross-border harvesting of reeds the consultative meeting was able to raise the interprovincial border issue. The Shandong side insisted that the borderline had already been fixed by State Council orders and that the disputed areas should be under Shandong province administration. Again, the Shandong side proposed a version of administrative re-adjustment program in which Peixian county transferred an area of 1.5–2.5 km or more of lakeside land to Weishan county. Shandong also insisted that the drainage from the lake drainage be under Shandong's administration. In contrast, the Jiangsu side disagreed, insisting that, following the administrative re-adjustment and the fact that the lake had already been divided into two parts by the Shandong dam, then the whole lake should be shared jointly by Shandong and Jiangsu provinces.[15]

Again, the differences between the two sides resulted in an inconclusive meeting that ended without any real conflict resolution.

5.3.2. The 'Inter-Ministerial Scheme'

In October 1980, two armed fights, this time between waring parties equipped with rifles and light machines guns, ended with four persons killed and 82 others wounded (see Table 5.1 for details). Realizing the critical status of the Lake Weishan, the State Council appointed the Ministry of Civil Affairs (MCA) and Ministry of Water Conservancy (MWC) to jointly investigate the situation. Team

---

[15] Ibid.

members included Liu Jinzhang of Department of Civil Affairs (of MCA), Fan Beitian of Department of Planning and Zhang Defu and Chen Chuankang of Department of Strategic Programming (both of MWC), and Tang Youngyuan of Huaihe River Administrative Commission. After the joint field-investigations, the MCA-MWC working group presented a report concerning the administrative re-delimitation on Lake Weishan. In this report, the group finally concluded that the 1953 delimitation scheme in which "the lakeside land was set as the interprovincial border" failed to take a full account of the changing natural conditions, and that the delimitation scheme was not in accord with proposals for economic development of the area, neither did it follow the conventional, and acceptable, models of administrative divisions. Moreover, the MCA–MWC group also proposed a new administrative re-adjustment scheme, known as the 'inter-Ministerial scheme,' or IMS. The main decisions of the IMS included proposals that determined:

(1) To set the border at the center of the lower area of the lake (that is, of the southern area from the dam), while the eastern and western parts of the border being under Shandong and Jiangsu provinces respectively;

(2) To set the border along the river of the lake-bank (shundi he) (from the dam to Yaolou River in the north), approximately with the eastern and western parts of the river under Shandong and Jiangsu provinces respectively; and

(3) For sake of the unified management of the dam, to set an area of one kilometer long from the dam as under the administration of Shandong province.[16]

In addition, the IMS also recommended that it was important: (1) to return to the old (pre-1953) interprovincial border, while keeping Weishan county under Shandong province; and (2) to put the upper and lower lakes to be under the jurisdictions of Shandong and Jiangsu provinces respectively.[17] With regard to the inter-Ministerial scheme, the State Council wrote in its official comments: "Conflicts have lasted for more than 20 years in this [Weishan] lake, which have not been resolved successfully. The inter-Ministerial scheme can resolve those problems fundamentally. Both provinces should, from the standpoints of long-run security and solidarity of the whole area, do their best jobs for the ideological

---

[16] Cited from MCA and MWC (1982).
[17] Ibid.

persuasion of the related counties and administrative localities, so as to resolve this issue smoothly." (State Council, 1981)

However, when the inter-Ministerial scheme was released, Shandong and Jiangsu provinces again reacted with different points of view. Jiangsu agreed it in principle, while requesting some supplementary revisions. Shandong rejected the scheme as saying that it would not solve the old problems; in effect it would result in an entire list of new ones. Specifically, Shandong argued that the scheme had four major drawbacks for it would:

(1) bring about difficulties for Weishan's fishermen, with about 40 thousands of those who lived at the lower lake becoming job-less;
(2) be disadvantageous for the construction and management of water conservancy, and to raise the contradictions between draining, storing water and construction of projects related to the lake;
(3) be disadvantageous for the lake-related production and fishery production in particular; and
(4) be disadvantageous for the administrative governance and public security of the whole area. [18]

In addition, Shandong province re-emphasized the effectiveness of the official document approved by the central government in 1953, insisting that, with the exception of some minor areas, the whole Lake Weishan area should be under the unified administration of Weishan county. Shandong's border re-adjustment scheme included the transfer of 109 villages on the western lakeside, or at least 30 villages with the closest proximity to the western lakeside, from Jiangsu province to Weishan county. [19] Since the views from both sides were once again in conflict, the inter-Ministerial scheme ended in failure.

In 1981, conflicts came again, commencing with lakeside reeds being burnt near border areas. On the evening of 22 September 1981, Peixian county authorities asked Weishan county officials to allow their police to enter a border area to investigate the causes of the fires. The Weishan administrators replied: "The lake is under the administration of Shandong province and the fires have already been investigated by officials from the Weishan side. No help is needed." [20] The vice-governors of Shandong and Jiangsu reached an oral agreement concerning the joint investigation into lakeside fires and joint control

---

[18] Based on the author's talks with county officials of Weishan county in Xiazhen township, Shandong province on 1 June 2000.
[19] Ibid.
[20] Cited from OLL (1998).

of border fires but, unfortunately, this agreement did not lead to the implementation of cordial relations between the two sides.

5.3.3. The 'Three Central Documents'

The Shandong–Jiangsu disputes over Lake Weishan have exhausted the energy of all provincial and local governments concerned. Unfortunately, there is still no sign of an end to the border conflicts. On 13 September 1983, three farmers were killed and one other was seriously wounded in a border fight. To resolve the conflict, the State Council dispatched yet another working group, this time led by Cui Naifu, Minister of the MCA. Members included Yang Zhenhui, vice-Minister of MWC, Wu Jiafu, vice Minister of Public Security, Lu Feng, vice-Governor of Shandong province, Ling Qiming, vice-Governor of Jiangsu province, Li Xianzhou, Department Chief of the MCA, Li Wen, Chief of Department of Civil Affairs of Shandong province, Shi Hongxian, Deputy Executive of Jining Administrative Region of Shandong province, Deputy Chief of Department of Civil Affairs of Jiangsu province, Dai Dengdong, Department Deputy Chief of MWC, Zhu Qun, Deputy Executive of Xuzhou Administrative Region of Jiangsu province, and Chen Leyin, vice-Magistrate of Weishan county of Shandong province. Before his departure from Beijing, on the afternoon of 22 January 1984 Cui met Vice-Premiers Wan Li and Tian Jiyun of the State Council. Wan Li pointed out: "In order to thoroughly resolve this problem, the State Council has made a definite decision. After having taken into account of all gains and losses, it seems better to put all disputed villages under the administration of Shandong province." (OLL, 1984) This speech, as Jiangsu provincial administrators complained, proved that the Lake Weishan disputes had been settled before the Cui Naifu-led group went to Lake Weishan.

On 30 April 1984, the CCP Central Committee and the State Council in an official document (zhongfa [84], official letter No. 11) approved the "Report on Issues Concerning the Resolution of Lake Weishan Disputes" presented by the working group. With regard to the lake-related resources, the Report suggests: "Areas where reeds and valliseria sprialis have been harvested by people of Peixian county without violence for the last three years may be kept unchanged, but should be under Weishan county administration." With regard to the disputed areas, the Report states: "Areas where there were armed conflicts within the last three years should be under the administration of Weishan county if villagers are dependent on the lake-related resources; if villagers are not dependent on lake resources then they should not be allowed to enter the lake to conduct any lake-related businesses." With regard to the issue concerning the administrative division of lakeside land, the Report notes: "the [interprovincial] border shall be set on the basis of the actual status of land cultivation in 1983." Besides, the issue of public security was specified to be "the unified responsibility of Weishan county"; in addition "the armed fights after 1978 should continue to be handled by Weishan county; and the fighters generally may not be prosecuted except for those who have committed intentional killings."[21]

In order to promote the implementation of the interprovincial re-allocation of the lakeside land and other lake-related resources, as well as on the border delimitation, the State Council approved in its official document (guofa [84], official letter No. 109) "The Second Report on Issues Concerning the Resolution of Lake Weishan Disputes." This report, presented by the State Council's working group, recommended that 14 disputed villages (which include Yangtang, Sunzhuang, Dongmingcun, Ximingcun, Liuying, Chaozhuang, Wangzhuang, Dawagongzhuang, Zhaolou, Zhaomiao, Zhangzhuang, Guanlou, Pangmeng-zhuang, and Zhongwagongzhuang) of Peixian county, Jiangsu province be transferred to Weishan county, Shandong province; but that the coal resources under Lake Weishan should still belong to Jiangsu. This was because Shandong is a much more energy resource rich province than Jiangsu. But this arrangement created yet another series of cross-border disputes. These will be examined in more detail in Section 5.4.3. In addition, the six border villages of Qianfeng'le, Houfeng'le, An'zhuang, Dianzi, Penglou, and Mazhuang in Jiangsu were granted their own provincial identity, responsible for their own administration, but villagers from these communities were not allowed to enter the lake area to conduct lake-related activities. Notice that Peixian county considered this decision as of unfair redistribution of productive and living materials from Jiangsu to Shandong provinces (OLL, 1985). Finally, the Report made two further declarations (1) the lake fisheries shall be under the unified administration of Weishan county; and (2) the maintenance of the western lake embankment shall be under the unified guidance and management of the Huaihe River Administrative Commission (the regional water resource management organ of the Ministry of Water Conservancy).[22]

With regard to the administrative division of the lakeside land and lake-related resources, the Administrative Office of the State Council (AOSC) issued another official document (document No. 61). In this document, the 10 km long section from Fangcun to the border between Peixian and Tongshan counties,

---

[21] Citied from State Council (1984a).
[22] See State Council (1984b).

about 10,000 mu reeds and 14,000 mu lakeside land and lake-related resources in the eastern part of the Beijing–Hangzhou Canal would be operated by Peixian county, while the rest would be operated by Weishan county; and about 7,000 mu lakeside land and lake-related resources along the lower reach from the dam (that is, from the Beijing–Hangzhou Canal in the west to the foot of Sidaodi in the east) would be shared by Peixian and Weishan counties under a proportionate allocation of two to one.[23]

The interprovincial division of lakeside land was based on the actual status of land cultivation in 1983, but that of the lake-related resources was based on what actually operated over the three years 1981 to 1983. These decrees were considered appropriate for the sake of protecting the benefits of the farmers while still following the established production schedules.[24] On September 8, 1984, the counties of Peixian and Weishan drafted a joint statement regarding attempts made towards the fulfilment of the objectives included in these decrees.[25] However, since the supervision of these objectives from higher governmental authorities has been ineffective, these central documents have not been implemented successfully.

The central government has now issued three high-level official documents relating to the resolution of disputes in the Lake Weishan region. The Weishan area has been the only interprovincial border area that has received serious attention from central government authorities in China. The major official documents on issues relating to Lake Weishan, from 1953 to 1998, can be found below in chronological order:[26]

1. Official Letter (zhengzhengbuzi No. 136), State Administrative Council of the People's Republic of China, 22 August 1953.
2. No. (67)173 Ordinance, State Council and the CCP Central Military Committee, 1967.
3. "Report Concerning the Scheme of Re-adjusting the Shandong–Jiangsu Border in Lake Weishan Area" (guanyu sulu liangsheng weishanhu diqu huajie fang'an de baogao), jointly by the Ministry of Civil Affairs (min[1981], No. 68) and Ministry of Water Conservancy ([1981]shuigui, No. 48), 1981.

---

[23] See AOSC (1985).
[24] Ibid.
[25] See PJWS (1984).
[26] *Source*: Provided by various government agencies of counties of Peixian (Jiangsu province) and Weishan (Shandong province).

4. "The State Council's Official Comments on 'Report Concerning the Scheme of Re-adjusting the Shandong–Jiangsu Border in Lake Weishan Area' of Ministry of Civil Affairs and Ministry of Water Conservancy" (guowuyuan dui minzhengbu, shuilibu 'guanyu sulu liangsheng weishanhu diqu huajie fang'an de baogao' de pishi), State Council, 1981.

5. "Report on Issues Concerning the Resolution of Lake Weishan Disputes" (guanyu jiejue weishanhu zhengyi wenti de baogao), the State Council's Dispatched Working Group to Lake Weishan, 9 April 1984.

6. The Second Report on Issues Concerning the Resolution of Lake Weishan Disputes" (guanyu jiejue weishanhu zhengyi de dierci baogao), presented by the State Council's dispatched working group, 23 August 1984.

7. Official Letter (zhongfa[1984], No. 11), CCP Central Committee, 30 April 1984.

8. Official Letter (guofa[1984], No. 109), State Council, 27 August 1984.

9. "Summary of the Negotiations Concerning the Fulfillment of the Documents Issued by the CCP Central Committee (zhongfa[1984], No. 11) and the State Council (guofa[1984], No. 109)" (guanyu guance zhixing zhongfa[1984] 11hao wenjian he guofa[1984] 109hao wenjian de shangtan jiyao), Peixian county, Shandong province and Weishan county, Shandong province, 8 September 1984.

10. "Notification on the Dispatching of the 'Report Presented by the Ministry of Civil Affairs on Issues Concerning the Resolution of the Scopes of the Lakeside Land and Lake-related Production between the Southern and Northern Lake Weishan'" (zhuanfa minzhengbu guanyu jiejue weishanhu nanbei liangduan hutian, huchan jingying fanwei wenti de baogao tongzhi), Official Document No. 61, Administrative Office of the State Council, 5 September 1985.

11. Official Letter No. 54, Government and CCP Committee of Jiangsu Province, 18 March 1992.

12. Official Letter of the Ministry of Geology and Minerals (dihan [1994], No. 318), 21 December 1994.

13. "Status Relating to the Cross-Provincial Exploitation of Datun Coal and Electricity Company and Xuzhou Coal Administration" (kuasheng kaicai de datun meidian gongsi, xuzhou kuangwuju youguan qingkuang), the Local Taxation Bureau, Shandong province, April 17, 1995.

14. "Letter Concerning Jiangsu's Sole Right over the Collection of Resources Taxation on the Datun Coal and Electricity Company" (guanyu jiangsu quanquan zhengshou datun meidian gongsi ziyuanshui de han),

suzhenghan [1995], No. 56, Government of Jiangsu province, March 1995.

15. "Emergent Request on Issues Concerning the Resources Taxation Levied by Shandong Province on Datun Coal and Electricity Company" (guanyu shandong sheng zhengshou datun meidian gongsi ziyuanshui wenti de jinji qingshi), Government of Peixian county, 1 November 1996.

16. "Request Concerning the Jiangsu Province's Collection of the Mining-Compensated Fees (MCFs) on Datun Coal and Electricity Company" (guanyu you jiangsu sheng zhengshou datum meidian gongsi kuangchan ziyuan bushangfei de shenqing), sucaiji [1997] No. 26, government of Jiangsu province.

17. "Report Concerning the Collection of the Mining-Compensated Fees on Datun Coal and Electricity Company" (guanyu zhengshou datum meidian gongsi suoshu ge meikuang kuangchan ziyuan bushangfei youguan yijian de baogao), ludifa [1997], No. 16, government of Shandong province.

18. "Letter on Opinions Concerning the Location of Collection of Taxation on Coal Resources in the Lake Weishan Area" (guanyu weishanhu diqu meitan ziyuanshui nashui didian de yijian de han), Ministry of Finance and State Taxation Bureau (caishuizi [1997], No. 55), 1997.

19. "Letter Replying to Issues Concerning the Collection of the Mining-Compensated Fees (MCFs) on the Datun Coal and Electricity Company" (guanyu zhengshou daun meidian gongsi kuangchan ziyuan bushangfei de youguan wenti de pifu), Ministry of Finance and Ministry of Geology and Minerals (caijizi [1997], No. 851), 21 November 1997.

20. "Report on the Work of the Delimitation between Peixian and Weishan Counties" (guanyu peiwei bianjie kanjie gongzuo de huibao), the Working Office of Lake Area, Peixian County, 17 February 1998.

21. "Report on Request of a Thorough Resolution of Jiangsu–Shandong Disputes over Lake Weishan" (guanyu qingqiu cedi jiejue sulu weishanhu maodun de baogao), peizhengbao [1998], No. 18, the government of Peixian county, 10 June 1998.

However, the fundamental problems of Lake Weishan have still not been resolved. Each side of the dispute will only accept the items favourable to its case and rejects the unfavorable conditions. For example, at the technical meeting on the administrative transfer of the disputed villages from Jiangsu to Shandong provinces (that is, the implementation of the No. 11 central document), held in Xuzhou city, Jiangsu province in 1984, Weishan county stated that the number of disputed villages is 38, while Peixian county argued that the figure had been overstated. Jiangsu province argued that "[this border re-adjustment scheme] disrupts the [Jiangsu's] draining and irrigating system that was established in the past, with most entrances and exits (eight of the ten rivers) being controlled by Shandong province." (OLL, 2000)

Some items in the three central documents are not well defined nor were they consistent with each other. As a result the decrees were not implemented. As Jiangsu provincial administrators argued, the governing principle that 'Wherever there is a conflict, the judgement of the administration of Shandong province will stand" had not solved the long running problems; rather, it was set to create new problems. For example, after 1984 when the administrative division was re-adjusted, the 64.2 km lakebank on the west side of Lake Weishan was divided into 16 separately administered sections between Shandong and Jiangsu provinces. Eight sections, with a total length of 23 km, were placed under Weishan county governance. Even worse, the 10 km long lakeside road from Datun to Hutun, both in Peixian county, was also cut into six separately administered sections (GPC, 1988). As a result, the Shandong–Jiangsu border on the western coast of Lake Weishan has been divided into an irregular administratively complex set of districts that are the basis for further discord and confusion (see Figure 4.2(a)). This will have further negative impacts on projects for the construction of water conservancy and communication infrastructure as well as on public security for the whole border area.

Just a few days prior to our first field trip to Weishan between 1–3 June 2000, an armed fight once again broke out between the local residents of the two provinces in the border region. This fighting resulted into the dislocation of communication between Weishan and Peixian counties. Our cross-border trips were also impeded by security problems. Fearing that their car might be detained by the Jiangsu side (Peixian county), Weishan county officials did not dare to send us beyond their border with Peixian county. Peixian's officials would not venture across to Weishan county to meet us. As a result, we had to transfer between the two cars by walking across the 'forbidden' border.

5.4. DEEPER CAUSES FOR DISCORD

The long-lasting conflicts have resulted from the inaccurate, changeable borderline between Shandong and Jiangsu provinces. In the Lake Weishan area, the interprovincial border is represented by lakeside land (hutian) boundaries set by the central government in 1953. Because this boundary line is subject to the changing levels of the water, conflict over the fluctuating dimensions of the lake and the lakeside land is the core element in the interprovincial borderline dispute. As a result, until a permanent solution is found, cross-border conflicts are unavoidable in the Lake Weishan area.

In addition to this geographical factor, political, economic and cultural factors have also been responsible for dissent.

5.4.1. Political and Institutional Causes

The experiences of both developed and developing countries in the post-World War II period have demonstrated that the success of a nation in promoting its social security and prosperity depends to a large extent on a comprehensive national legal system and effective jurisprudence.

China's current political and legal systems have been deeply influenced by long periods of feudalism, which are not consistent with a market system.[27] Recently, China has made efforts to improve its legal system on the interprovincial relations, but further progresses are still needed. For example, China does not have any constitutional clauses which specifically prohibit the establishment of barriers to interprovincial commerce. Many rules and regulations relating to the removal of local business blockades have had little influence on the policy-makers at provincial and local levels.[28] Although regulations concerning the resolution of border disputes between administrative regions have been adopted and then revised by the State Council in 1981 and 1988, respectively, many articles in the regulations are unclear and difficult to enforce.[29]

As mentioned in Section 5.1, the whole lake area had been under the sole jurisdiction of Shandong province as early as in 1953. The central government's initial intend was based on a logical redistribution of water resources between the two provinces. This was based on resource calculated over the whole province, not just the Weishan region. However, since most of the water resources in Jiangsu province have been distributed in the southern and central areas, the northern areas, especially those bordered with Shandong province, have been dependent on Lake Weishan for fresh water supplies. In addition, due to China's lack of petroleum, coal exploitation has been for a long period given critical attention by both central and provincial governments. According to the final resolution of Lake Weishan disputes, all underground coal resources were granted

---

[27] For example, about 220 Chinese laws are incompatible with the World Trade Organization rules and will have to be changed (Reti, 2001, pp. 17-19).

[28] See, for example, State Council (1980; 1982; 1986; 1990), and NPC (1993).

[29] See State Council (1981; 1988) for details about these regulations.

to Jiangsu province (see Section 5.3.3). Once again, this decision was based on estimation of the poorer resource base held by Jiangsu. Shandong is considered a relatively resource rich province. However, it must be noted that, without appropriate institutional building and interprovincial coordination, the above arrangements could cause further harm to the management of the cross-border resources in Lake Weishan.

For a long period, especially during the Cultural Revolution, Chinese society had little respect for rule of law. According to Article 132 of the 1979 version of the Criminal Law of the People's Republic of China (NPC, 1979), "A person who commits murder with intend may be sentenced to death, to life imprisonment, or to between 10 years of fixed-term imprisonment but no less than three years in prison. If a person commits manslaughter the sentence should be no more than 10 years in prison." However, this Article had not been put into effective with regard to the armed fights in the Lake Weishan region (the weapons stockpiled or used by the border fighters are listed at the last column of Table 5.1). Moreover, according to the current Criminal Law, "Whoever illegally manufactures, trades, transports, mails, or stockpiles guns, ammunition, or explosives is to be sentenced to no less than three years but no more than 10 years of fixed-termed imprisonment; or no less than 10 years of imprisonment, life imprisonment, or death if the consequences are serious."[30]

During the time of our fieldtrip to Lake Weishan, we were told that the people who had been responsible for killing other fighters in border disputes had actually been treated meritoriously by their respective sides. They either remained at large or, for the sake of calming down the state of cross-border tensions, had been only punished with trivial rebukes or fines. Many were later appointed to important posts. For example, during the dispute-resolution in 1973, Duan Yongkan – General Secretary of the CCP branch of Dajuan Brigade (an administrative unit of Weishan county) – was known to have led a cross-border fight in which four people were killed and 55 wounded (see Table 5.1). A local court in Shandong province sentenced him to three years of fixed-term imprisonment. Duan was later released ahead of time and he continued to hold the post as Party General Secretary. In 1981, he was again involved in a border conflict.[31]

---

[30] See NPC (1997, Article 125).
[31] See OLL (1998).

5.4.2. Provincial Economic Reforms

Since the late 1970s, public finance, as an important component of the Chinese economic system, has undergone a series of reforms on the central-local relations. The main goals of these reforms were to decentralize the fiscal structure and to strengthen the incentive for local governments to collect more revenue for themselves. Obviously, the economic decentralization has been largely responsible for China's current economic success.[32] However, this kind of reform has also had negative impacts on interprovincial relations. For example, in order to protect local market and revenue sources, it has become very common in China for provinces to restrict imports (exports) from (to) other provinces by levying high, if informal, taxes and by creating non-tariff barriers on commodities whose production is seen as important to their provincially 'domestic' economies.[33] This unfair competition between provinces has become a fierce 'battleground' in border-regions and there were numerous examples of 'trade embargoes' or 'commodity wars' between provinces over essential items, such as rice, wool, tobacco, soy beans, and mineral products.[34]

Setting aside the period of the Cultural Revolution during the early 1970s, fighting was most serious at Lake Weishan during the 1980s (see Table 5.1). This was due to the fact that the farmers residing around Lake Weishan had more incentives to cultivate lakeside land when the Household Responsibility System (HRS) was introduced following the People's Commune System (PCS) of collectivization. For example, the average output value for the cultivation of the lakeside land had been approximately 2,000 yuan per *mu*, with few inputs in fertilizers and pesticides and almost no need of arable management. If cultivation included both agricultural and aquatic productions, the average output level of the lakeside land would increase additionally.[35] From 1982 to 2002, the outputs of grains and aquatic products increased by the annual rates of 2.56 percent and 8.63 percent respectively. In some disputed areas along the western coast of the lake (in the proximity of the interprovincial border), the growth rates were much higher. For example, as shown in Table 5.3, the output of aquatic products in Xiping and Zhaomiao townships increased drastically by 19.69 percent and 15.80 percent respectively from 1986 to 2001, much higher than that in Weishan county as a whole (8.63 percent).

---

[32] See, for example, Oi (1992, pp. 99-129), Wong (1992), Shirk (1993), and Jin *et al.* (2001).
[33] See, for example, Shen and Dai (1990, pp. 1-13), and Li (1993, pp. 23–36).
[34] More detailed evidences may be found in Sun (1993, pp. 95–104), Feng (1993, pp. 87–94), and Goodman (1994, p. 1–20).
[35] Source: Office of Lakeside Land Administration, Peixian county.

**Table 5.3. The imbalanced cultivations in selected disputed areas at Lake
Weishan**

Area	Year	Population ('000 persons)	Area of cultivated land (ha)	Output of grains (ton)	Output of aquatic products (ton)
Xiping township	1986	7429	773	3276	34
	2001	9299	696	4689	504
	AGR (%)	1.51	-0.70	2.42	19.69
Zhaomiao township	1986	11169	1027	4803	78
	2001	14423	954	5533	704
	AGR (%)	1.72	-0.53	0.95	15.80
Gaolou township	1982	15885	2140	3850	3500
	2001	20586	3976	20468	11450
	AGR (%)	1.37	4.52	9.19	6.44
Weishan county	1982	509212	50053	152335	11848
	2002	685200	54213	252800	62000
	AGR (%)	1.50	0.57	2.56	8.63

Notes: (1) AGR=annual growth rate. (2) Xiping and Zhaomiao townships were
administratively transferred from Jiangsu to Shandong provinces in 1985.
Source: Calculated by the author based on the data provided by Statistical Department of
Weishan county, Shandong province.

Even more dramatic was the eight fold increase in the area of cultivated land.
The output in grain harvesting of Gaolou township between 1982 and 2001, was
almost four times that of Weishan as a whole. Given that the total size of land,
water, and other lake-related resources was constant, the interprovincial
redistribution of these resources must be following a zero-sum game. Along with
the cross-border competitions for capturing the resources at Lake Weishan, the
frequency of disputes and armed fighting increased accordingly.

The economic decentralization also provided incentives for the provincial and
local governments in Shandong and Jiangsu provinces to compete with each other
for the collection of local taxes and fees for cross-border coal exploitation. Below
is an example in this regard.

Located at the township of Datun, Peixian county, the Datun Coal and
Electricity Corporation (DCEC) was built by the Shanghai municipal government
in 1970. It includes a thermal power plant, a railroad, and four coalmines
(Longdong, Yaoqiao, Xuzhuang and Kongzhuang , with an annual output of
4,000,000 tons of raw coal). The initial reason for the construction of these
coalmines was to meet the urgent demand for electric energy in Shanghai
municipality. However, as the DCEC was entitled to exploit coal resources under
the Lake Weishan area, it was affected by the Shandong–Jiangsu border disputes.

Faced with operational difficulties, the Shanghai municipal government transferred this Corporation to the Ministry of Coal Industry in Beijing in the early 1980s. The Ministry was abolished subsequently in 1998, and the DCEC was made a sub-company of a state-owned coal enterprise in Beijing.

Although the central government has granted underground resources to Jiangsu province, it did not specifically mention the collection of taxes and fees levied on the exploitation of these resources, nor were the relevant laws and regulations issued during that period. This was not a problem in the pre-reform era when the Chinese economy had followed a centrally planned system. However, in the reform period it has brought about interprovincial disputes, as the Chinese economy has been increasingly decentralized. With regard to the cross-border collection of taxes and fees on coal exploitation, Jiangsu and Shandong provinces submitted proposals separately to the Ministry of Geology and Minerals (MGM) in late 1993 and early 1994.[36]

On 21 December 1994, the MGM replied to the two provincial bureaus of geology and minerals (BGMs) and granted Shandong province the right to collect 30 percent (Longdong coalmine) and 45 percent (Yaoqiao, Xuzhuang and Kongzhuang coalmines) of the Mining-Compensated Fees (MCFs), and Jiangsu province to collect the rest.[37] Shandong and Jiangsu province reacted to this decision differently. While Shandong officials were collecting their MCF allocations, the Bureau of Local Taxation of Shandong province submitted a new proposal to the State Taxation Bureau (STB). In this proposal, dated on 17 April 1995, Shandong provincial administrators stated that because the coal exploitation of the DCEC's four coalmines extended across the border of Shandong province, the MGM had granted Shandong and Jiangsu the right to collect the MCFs separately; moreover, since resources-tax had much similarity with MCFs, it also should be shared by Shandong and Jiangsu provinces proportionally (LTB, 1995).

The Jiangsu provincial officials rejected both the MGM's decision and Shandong's new proposal (GJP, 1995). Jiangsu's gave the following reasons for rejecting the decision: (1) the ownership of the underground resources had been granted to Jiangsu province, this had already been settled according to the Jiangsu local government; (2) during its coal exploration and exploitation phases, the DCEC received a great deal of assistance from Jiangsu province with regard to land utilization, migration, employment, the supply of living facilities, public security, and environmental protection; and (3) Shandong province did not assist with the operation of the DCEC, even though its local villagers had already been

---

[36] See State Council (1993; 1994) for details.
[37] See the official letter of the Ministry of Geology and Minerals (dihan [1994], No. 318), 21 December 1994.

compensated properly for their damages and losses in relation to the coal exploitation (GPC, 1996). Realizing the critical emergency of this issue, the MGM forwarded Jiangsu's request to the Ministry of Civil Affairs (MCA), the State Taxation Bureau (STB) and the Ministry of Finance (MOF) for comments, before submitting it to the State Council for final assessment.

The interprovincial taxation disputes had lasted for four years before the MOF, MGM and STB jointly issued a final resolution on 21 November 1997: resource-tax should be solely collected by Jiangsu province; and MCFs should be collected by Jiangsu province and be equally shared by the central government and Jiangsu provincial government (MOF and STB, 1997; and MOF and MGM, 1997). Shandong province would not benefit from the interprovincial taxation disputes.

5.4.3. Cultural Influences

Most of China's provinces are considerable political and economic systems in their own right. The social, economic and cultural differences between these provinces have long been part of the defining characteristic of China's political sphere for over two thousand years. Chinese culture is not homogeneous across provinces, in terms of ethnic and linguistic groups. As a result, the chance of the adoption of a common standard and interprovincial coordination is slight.

During the field research carried out in the Lake Weishan area, we noted that local officials doubted about the fairness of the central government's final decisions on resolutions of the Lake Weishan disputes. Their most serious concern was that those key central government officials who had provincial ties to either Shandong or Jiangsu were inclined to make resolutions in favor of one side or the other. According to our talks with the local officials of Peixian county, the final decision made by the central government concerning the resolution of the Weishan lake disputes (see Section 5.3.3) was seen as unfair by Jiangsu provincial authorities since the top decision-makers, Wan Li and Tian Jiyun – both held the position of vice premiership of the State Council during the 1980s – were born in Shandong province (see Table 5.4). The speech given by Comrade Wan Li, as Jiangsu officials complained, had set the scene for the final resolution of the disputes in 1983. Wan Li pointed out: "In order to find a thorough resolution to this problem, the State Council has made a fairly definite decision. After having taken into account of all gains and losses, it seems better to put all disputed villages under the administration of Shandong province."[38]

Table 5.4. Who's who in the resolution process of the Lake Weishan disputes

Name	Title	Native place	Year(s) of resolution involved
Zhou En'lai	Premier of SC	Jiangsu	1967
Du Ping	Commissar of NMD	Jiangxi	1967
Zhang Bangying	Minister of MCA	Shanxi	1980–81
Qian Zhengying	Minister of MWC	Zhejiang	1980–81
Wan Li	Vice-Premier of SC	Shandong	1983–84
Tian Jiyun	Vice-Premier of SC	Shandong	1983–84
Cui Naifu	Minister of MCA	Jiangxi	1983–84

Notes: SC=the State Council; MCA=Ministry of Civil Affairs; MWC=Ministry of Water Conservancy; NMD=Nanjing Military District of the Central Military Committee of Communist Party of China.

In our meetings with the local officials in Peixian county, the Jiangsu side stated that, since some key central officials were natives of Shandong province, Jiangsu province had been placed in a disadvantageous position. By contrast, there was also a growing fear from the Shandong side that the resolution of the local disputes had favored Jiangsu province since, during the 1990s, more key central government officials came from southern China. There was a joke released by Chen Xitong, former Major of Beijing municipality and then member of Politburo of CCP's Central Committee during the early 1990s. When asked by his friends about the content of Jiang Zemin-sponsored meeting of Politburo of CCP's Central Committee that he just attended, he burbled: "I cannot hear a word, since they only spoke in Shanghai tone [a sub-category of Wu dialect that has been widely applied in southern Jiangsu and the Yangtze river delta areas]." For example, with regard to their victory in the resolution of the interprovincial taxation disputes (as discussed in Section 5.4.2), the Jiangsu officers admitted in an internal, confidential, report that they had done 'hard and meticulous works.' (WOLA, 1998)

The key issues that were not included in the final resolution were: (1) the legality of the ownership transfer of Shandong's underground resources to Jiangsu province; and (2) the entitlement by Shandong province to levy taxes and fees on

---

[38] Cited from OLL (1984).

the exploitation of resources underlying its territory. For instance, Article 12 of "Temporary Regulations Concerning the Resource Taxation of the People's Republic of China" (Beijing, State Council, No. 139 document, 25 December 1993) states that: "Tax payers shall pay taxes to the taxation bureau in charge of places from which the taxed products originate."

During our stay at Weishan, we saw first hand the deep mistrust felt between both sides when a member of the reception staff of the Magistrate Office of Weishan county saw the two Chinese characters 'da tun' in the name card of our team member. The word 'Datun' written on the card referred to a place of Beijing not a locality in Peixian county. The receptionist was made immediately suspicious of the credentials of the field team. In addition, some border-related questions were raised by my accompanying member who used Wu-style Mandarin in his speech (Wu is a Chinese dialect widely applied in southern Jiangsu province). This led to further uneasiness in the approach of some Weishan county officials.

Fortunately, our survey went smoothly, since we stated time and again that our inquiry was for academic purpose. Nevertheless, a private comment by a Deputy Magistrate reminded us of the prospect of the final resolution of the interprovincial border disputes: "We don't care which province administers Weishan lake and the county. It is also OK for us if Weishan county belongs to Jiangsu province."[39]

5.5. IS THERE ANY SOLUTION?

The Shandong–Jiangsu border disputes have resulted in a long history of human suffering and environmental damage. Any situation as complex as this can rarely be found in any other disputed interprovincial border areas in mainland China.

The border disputes have been fought over lakeside land, submerged resources, drainage and irrigation project, water conservancy projects, communication infrastructure and public security. The disputes have received the urgent attention from many ministries including the Ministry of Civil Affairs, the Ministry of Geology and Minerals, the Ministry of Public Security, the Ministry of Water Conservancy, the Ministry of Finance, the State Taxation Bureau, and even the State Council and the CCP's Central Committee.

---

[39] Cited from a private conversation at a banquet hosted by the government of Weishan county in Xiazhen town, 2 June 2000.

For decades, the border conflicts have peaked during periods of seasonal calamity. It has been recognized that: "A great drought occurred in the lake for every eight or nine years; this 'drought' has usually lasted for three years and during this period conflicts have reached their highest levels." (WOLA (1998) The interprovincial conflicts have wasted energy and resources at all levels of provincial and local government.

This has impeded the economic and social development of the lake area as a whole. In Weishan county, the position of magistrate deputy has been established principally for the purpose of dealing with border conflicts and related matters; while in Peixian county, an office has been established to take charge of the lakeside land cultivation and the border-related affairs.

Indeed, the economic separation between Shandong and Jiangsu provinces has become particularly serious during the current reform era when the Chinese economy has been transformed from a centrally planned system into a decentralized administrative model.

Even worse, Shandong and Jiangsu provinces both have different policies relating to issues such as population control, market management, pricing, collection of taxes and fees, public security, and agricultural and industrial production. This cross-border diversity provides further disincentives for the sustainable development of the Weishan lake area.

Given the difficulties in the current administrative arrangements, is there an alternative to the present situation of continual interprovincial border disputes?

Mainland China's 31 provinces (autonomous regions, autonomous municipalities) average about one-third of a million square kilometers of land area with more than 40 million people, each equivalent to a European country in population and land area. Of course, it is not possible to find an optimal size for each of these provinces. However, we can conclude from the Chinese data (see Table 5.5) that the four provinces of Jiangsu, Shandong, Henan and Anhui surrounding the Weishan lake area are too large both in terms of population, land area, or economic fundamentals to be single provinces.

In short, the establishment of a new province (or provincial unit) in the border areas of Jiangsu, Shandong, Henan and Anhui provinces could serve two major functions:

o   First, increase the efficiency of spatial administration over Lake Weishan and the adjacent areas by transferring the multitude of administrative system into a unitary administrative structure; and

o   Second, achieve more economies of scale for provincial administration by separating the marginal border areas out of the over-sized provinces.

Table 5.5. Are the provinces surrounding the Lake Weishan area too large in size?

Province	Population[a] (000 persons)	Land area (000' km^2)	Economic size[b] (000' (persons×km^2)$^{1/2}$)	Distance from Weishan to provincial capital (km)
Henan	95550.0	160.0	3910.0	349
Shandong	90410.0	150.0	3682.6	317
Jiangsu	73550.0	100.0	2712.0	346
Anhui	63280.0	130.0	2868.2	296
Provincial Average of China[c]	40897.7	299.8	2762.8	

Notes:

[a]: As of the end of 2001 (Source: NBS, 2002).

[b]: Calculated by the geometric mean of 'Population' and 'Land Area'.

[c]: A total number of 31 provinces, autonomous regions and municipalities (except Hong Kong, Macau and Taiwan) are included.

The Chinese government has already set an example in the case of Sichuan – the most populous province with a population of more than 100 million. In 1997 a new provincial unit, the Chongqing municipality, was created. In 1988, Hainan Island, previously a marginalized area of Guangdong province, became a separate province. Since then, all the new provinces have worked quite well in promoting their provincial economic identities.[40]

It should be noted that the establishment of the new province in the border regions of Jiangsu, Shandong, Henan and Anhui provinces will not guarantee that all the border-related problems will be solved. Nevertheless, it would transform the inter-provincial border disputes into a set of issues that could reasonably be solved by a single province administration. In such a case, the question "Who owns Lake Weishan?" will no longer be part of an unsolved interprovincial equation!

---

[40] Based on the data of NBS (1996, 2002), we can find that from 1992 to 1995 the provincial economy of Sichuan lagged behind the Chinese economy as a whole; during 1998 and 2001, however, both of the two new provincial economies of Chongqing and Sichuan became more robust than the Chinese economy.

APPENDICES

A1. A LIST OF MAJOR POLITICAL AND ECONOMIC REFORMS IN CHINA

Year/M/D	Organizer(s)	Program
1978/12/18	Third Plenum of the 11th CCPCC	'Decision of the CCPCC Concerning the Reform of Economic System'
1979	NPC	'Law of the People's Republic of China Concerning the Joint Ventures with Chinese and Foreign Investment'
1979	CCPCC and State Council	Guangdong and Fujian provinces were granted with 'special policies and flexible measures' in foreign economic affairs.
1979/12/26	People's Congress of Guangdong province	Shenzhen next to Hong Kong, Zhuhai next to Macau, and Santou were designed as the SEZs, to experiment a market-oriented economy.
1980	State Council	Starting of the fiscal contract system
1980/8/26	NPC	Xiamen in Southeast Fujian province vis-à-vis Taiwan became a SEZ
1980/9	CCPCC and State Council	Household Responsibility System (HRS)
1984	State Council	'Provisional Regulations for the Management of 'Small-volume' Border Trade'
1984/4	CCPCC and the State Council	Design of 14 coastal open cities

Appendix A1. (Continued)

Year/M/D	Organizer(s)	Program
1984/5/10	State Council	'Provisional Regulations on the Enlargement of Autonomy of State-owned Industrial Enterprises'
1984/10/21	CCPCC	'Decision of the CCPCC Concerning the Reform of Economic Structure'
1985/2	State Council	The Yangtze River, Pearl River and South Fujian were approved as coastal economic development zones
1986	State Council	Regulations of Issues Concerning the Extensive Regional Economic Cooperation
1986/12	NPC	'Bankruptcy Law Concerning the SOEs'
1986/12	State Council	Encouraging the SOEs to adopt the contract system.
1988/3	State Council	Liaodong and Shandong peninsulas and Bohai Basin area were allowed to open up to the outside world
1988/4	NPC	Hainan province was approved as a SEZ with even more flexible policies than other SEZs
1990/4	CCPCC and the State Council	Shanghai's Pudong area was granted to enjoy some of the SEZ's mechanisms
1991	Yunnan province	'Provisional Regulations Concerning the Border Trade'
1992/7/14	Tibet autonomous region	'Resolutions Concerning the Further Reform and Opening up to the Outside World'
1991/4/20	Inner Mongolia autonomous region	'Resolution of Some Issues Concerning the Extension of Open-door and Promotion of Economic Development'
1992	State Council	'Notification Concerning the Further Opening up of the Four Frontier Cities of Heihe, Shuifenhe, Hunchun and Manzhouli'
1992/1/25	Office of Custom, PRC	'Measures Concerning the Supervision and Favourable Taxation for the People-to-People Trade in Sino–Myanmar Border'

Appendix A1. (Continued)

Year/M/D	Organizer(s)	Program
1992/2/9	Xinjiang autonomous region	'Notification of Promoting the Trade and Economic Cooperation with the Neighbouring and Eastern European Countries'
1992/6	State Commission for Restructuring the Economic Systems	'Provisional Regulations on Joint-Stock Companies'
1992/6	State Council	'Notification Concerning the Further Opening up of the Five Frontier Cities and Towns of Nanning, Kunming, Pingxiang, Ruili, and Hekou'
1992/6	Heilongjiang province	'Some Favourable Policies and Economic Autonomy Authorized to the Frontier Cities of Heihe and Shuifenhe'
1992/7/22	State Council	'Regulations on the Transformation of the Operating Mechanisms of State-owned Industrial Enterprises'
1993/11	Third Plenum of the 14th CCPCC	Establishment of the Modern Enterprise System
1993/11/14	Third Plenum of the 14th CCPCC	'Decision of the CCPCC on Several Issues Concerning the Establishment of a Socialist Market Economic Structure'
1994	People's Bank of China	Separation of banking from policy lending; reducing of the number of the central bank's regional braches from 30 or more to only six
1994	State Council	Introduction of 'tax-sharing system' into all provinces
1994/1/1	People's Bank of China	Establishment of a new unitary and floating exchange-rate system
1995/9	Fifth Plenum of the Fourteenth CCPCC	Policy of grasping the large and releasing the small SOEs
1998/3	The Ninth NPC	Amendment was to Article 6 of the Chinese Constitution: 'public, instead of state, ownership as the main form of ownership of the means of production'

Appendix A1. (Continued)

Year/M/D	Organizer(s)	Program
1999	State Council	Debt-equity swap scheme (zhai zhuan gu) in four large state-owned banks
2000/4/1	People's Bank of China	Adoption of 'real name' banking system
2001/11	WTO	China's access to TWO
2004/4	State Council	The abolishment of agricultural tax within 3 years
2003/12	State Council	Transformation of Bank of China and China Construction Bank into joint stock ownership
2008/7	State Council	Privatization of forestland for 70 years of tenure in selected areas
2008/8	People's Bank of China	More flexible foreign exchange policies
2008/10	Third Plenum of the 17th CCPCC	De facto land privatization in rural areas

A2. SPECIFICATION TO THE MODEL ON SYSTEM DYNAMICS

*   DYNAMO Equations

L   CGI.K=CGI.J+DT*(SOR.JK)
N   CGI=I0

CURRENT LEVEL OF INSTITUTION

R   SOR.KL=Q.K*(EGI-CGI.K)/T
C   EGI=1.0

SPEED OF REFORM

L   Y.K=Y.J+DT*EG.JK

INCOME LEVEL

N   Y=Y0
R   EG.KL=40*SOR.KL+0.2*FDI.K

ECONOMIC GROWTH

A   FDI.K=0.05*Y.K*O*IE.K

FORMATION OF FDI FLOWS

L   PS.K=PS.J+DT*DPS.JK
N   PS=1.001 SUPPOSE PS=1 WHEN TIME=0
R   DPS.KL=CC.K*EG.KL-5.0*SOR.KL-0.03*O
A   CC.K=2/Y0
A   Q1.K=MIN(PS.K-1,0)
A   Q2.K=MAX(PS.K-1,0)
A   Q.K=(Q2.K-Q1.K)/(PS.K-1)

REFORM MECHANISM

L   IE.K=IE.J+DT*DIE.JK
N   IE=1.0
R   DIE.KL=0.01*EG.KL+0.05*PS.K

INVEST ENVIRONMENT

C   I0=0.3 INITIAL GOOD INSTITUTION
C   O=1.0 OPEN-DOOR POLICY
C   Y0=100 INITIAL INCOME LEVEL
C   T=10 LENGTH OF TIME FOR REFORM

POLICY VARIABLES

SAVE CGI,Y
SPEC DT=1/LENGTH=40/SAVPER=1.

ABBREVIATIONS

AMC	asset-management company
AOSC	Administrative Office of the State Council
BB	Big bang
BSR	backstage ruler
CCP	Chinese Communist Party
CCPCC	Chinese Communist Party Central Committee
CEO	chief executive officer
CPE	centrally planned economy
CPPCC	Chinese People's Political Consultative Congress
DCEC	Datun Coal and Electricity Corporation
DYNAMO	dynamic model
ETDZ	economic and technological development zone
FDI	foreign direct investment
FSU	former Soviet Union
GDP	gross domestic product
GR	gradual reform
HRS	household responsibility system
IB	incumbent bureaucrats
IMS	inter-Ministerial scheme
MCA	Ministry of Civil Affairs
MCF	Mining-Compensated Fee
MDEs	mutual deterrence equilibria
MGM	Ministry of Geology and Minerals
MOF	Ministry of Finance
MWC	Ministry of Water Conservancy
NBS	National Bureau of Statistics of China

NIE	newly industrialized economy
NPC	National People's Congress
PBC	People's Bank of China
PCS	people's commune system
PRC	People's Republic of China
RMB	renminbi, Chinese currency
SARS	severe acute respiratory syndrome
SD	system dynamics
SEZ	special economic zone
SOE	state-owned enterprise
STB	State Taxation Bureau
WTO	World Trade Organization
ZBM	Zibo Mining Group

REFERENCES

Aghion, P. and O. Blanchard (1994), 'On the Speed of Transition in Central Europe', *National Bureau for Economic Research Macroeconomics Annual*, pp. 283–319.

AOSC (1985), 'Notification on the Dispatching of the "Report Presented by the Ministry of Civil Affairs on Issues Concerning the Resolution of the Scope of the Lakeside Land and Lake-related Production between the Southern and Northern Lake Weishan"' (zhuanfa minzhengbu guanyu jiejue weishanhu nanbei liangduan hutian, huchan jingying fanwei wenti de baogao tongzhi), Official Document No. 61, Administrative Office of the State Council (AOSC), 5 September 1985.

Åslund, A. (1991), 'Principles of Privatization', in L. Csaba (ed.), *Systemic Change and Stabilization in Eastern Europe*, Aldershot: Dartmouth, pp. 17–31.

Baokan Wenzhai (1989), 'The Armed Disputes in China's Internal Borders' (zhongguo bianjie da xiedou), *The Digest of Newspapers and Magazines*, 13 June, p. 4.

Bates, R., A. Greif, M. Levi, J-L. Rosenthal, and B. Weingast (1998), *Analytic Narratives*, Princeton, NJ: Princeton University Press.

Baum, R. (1994), *Burying Mao: Chinese Politics in the Age of Deng Xiaoping*, Princeton: Princeton University Press.

Berg, A. and J. Sachs (1992), 'Structural Adjustment and International Trade in Eastern Europe: The Case of Poland', *Economic Policy*, vol. 14, 117–74.

Boycko, M. (1992), 'When Higher Incomes Reduce Welfare: Queues, Labour Supply, and Macroeconomic Equilibrium in Socialist Economies', *Quarterly Journal of Economics*, vol. 107, 907–20.

Cai, F., D. Wang, and M. Wang (2002), 'China's Regional Specialization in the Course of Gradual Reform', *The Economic Research* (in Chinese), No. 9, 24–30.

Campos, N.F., and F. Coricelli (2002), 'Growth in Transition: What We Know, What We Don't and What Should', *Journal of Economic Literature*, vol. XL (September), 793–836.

CCPCC (1984), 'Decision of the CCPCC Concerning the Reform of Economic Structure', Beijing: the Third Plenum of the 12th CCPCC, Beijing, 21 October.

CCPCWC and PGWC (1998), 'An Outline of Report Concerning the Environmental Protection Work on the Four Southern Lakes' (guanyu nansihu huanbao gongzuo de huibao tigang), the CCP Committee of Weishan County (CCPCWC) and the People's Government of Weishan County (PGWC), 29 December 1998.

Chan, J. (2002), 'Chinese Communist Party to Declare Itself Open to the Capitalist Elite', available at: http://www.wsws.org/articles/2002/nov2002/chin-n13.shtml.

Chen, R. (1993), *The Craze of Xiahai* (xiahai kuangchao), Beijing: Tuanjie Chubanshe.

Chi, F. (2000), 'The WTO Accession and the Second Reform in China', *Business Management*, No. 11, 11–12.

Cihai (1999), Shanghai: Shanghai Cishu Publishing House

Corbet, H. (1996), 'Issues in the Accession of China to the WTO System', *Journal of Northeast Asian Studies*, vol. 15, No. 3.

Day, R.H. (1985), 'Dynamics Systems Theory and Complicated Economic Behaviors', *Environment and Planning*, vol. 12, pp. 55–64.

De Melo, M., C. Denizer, A. Gleb and S. Tenev (1997), 'Circumstances and Choice: the Role of Initial Condition and Politics in Transition Economies', *Policy Research Working Paper* No. 1866, Washington DC: The World Bank.

Demurger, S., J.D. Sachs, W.T. Woo, S. Bao, G. Cheng and A. Mellinger (2002), 'Geography, Economic Policy, and Regional Development in China', NBER Working Paper 8897.

Deng X. (1992), 'The Key Points of the Speeches in Wuchang, Shenzhen, Zhuhai, Shanghai, etc.' (zai in wuchang, shenzhen, zhuhai, shanghai deng di de jianghua yiaodian), in Literature Editing Committee of CCPCC (ed.), *Selected Works of Deng Xiaoping* (Deng Xiaoping wenxue), Beijing: The People's Press, pp. 370–83.

Dewatripont, M. and G. Roland (1992a), 'Economic Reform and Dynamic Political Constraints', *Review of Economic Studies*, vol. 59, 703–30.

Dewatripont, M. and G. Roland (1992b), 'The Virtues of Gradualism and Legitimacy in the Transition to a Market Economy', *Economic Journal*, vol. 102, 291–300.

Dewatripont, M. and G. Roland (1995), 'The Design of Reform Packages under Uncertainty', *American Economic Review*, vol. 85, 1207–23.

Dittmer, L., and Y. Wu (1993), 'The Political Economy of Reform Leadership in China: Macro and Micro Informal Politics Linkages', Paper presented to the Annual Meeting of the Association of Asian Studies, Los Angles.

Economic News, 11 February 1987; 21 December 1988, in Chinese.

Fewsmith, J. (1999), *China Since Tian'anmen: The Politics of Transition*, Cambridge: Cambridge University Press.

Fidrmuc, J. and A. G. Noury (2003), 'Interest Groups, Stakeholders, and the Distribution of Benefits and Costs of Reform', Thematic Paper, Washington DC: GDN.

Fischer, S. and A. Gelb (1991), 'The Process of Socialist Economic Transformation', *Journal of Economic Perspectives*, vol. 5, 91–105.

Forrester, J.W. (1959), 'Advertising: A Problem in Industrial Dynamics', *Harvard Business Review*, March–April, vol. 37(2), 100–10.

Forrester, J.W. (1969), *Industrial Dynamics*, Cambridge, MA: The MIT Press.

Frydman, R. and A. Rapaczynski (1994), *Privatization in Eastern Europe: Is the State Withering Away?* London: Central European University Press.

Garnaut, R. (1999), 'Introduction', in R. Garnaut and L. Song (eds.), *China: Twenty Years of Reform*, Canberra: Asia Pacific Press, pp. 1–20.

Garnaut, R. and Y. Huang (1995), 'China and the Future International Trading Systems', in *China and East Asia Trade Policy*, Pacific Economic Papers, No. 250, Australia–Japan Research Center, Australian National University.

Gilley, B. (2004), 'The 'End of Politics' in Beijing', *The China Journal*, No. 51, 115–35.

GJP (1995), 'Letter Concerning Jiangsu's Sole Right over the Collection of Resources Taxation on the Datun Coal and Electricity Company' (guanyu jiangsu quanquan zhengshou datun meidian gongsi ziyuanshui de han), suzhenghan [1995], No. 56, Government of Jiangsu province (GJP), March 1995.

Goodman, D.S.G. (1997), 'China in Reform: The View from the Provinces', in D.S.G. Goodman (ed.), *China's Provinces in Reform—Class, Community and Political Culture*, London: Rutledge.

Gottmann, J. (1973), *The Significance of Territory*, Charlottesville: University of Virginia Press.

GPC (1988), 'Report on Request of a Thorough Resolution of Jiangsu–Shandong Disputes over Lake Weishan' (guanyu qingqiu cedi jiejue sulu weishanhu maodun de baogao), peizhengbao [1998], No. 18, the government of Peixian county (GPC), 10 June 1998.

GPC (1996), 'Emergent Request on Issues Concerning the Resources Taxation Levied by Shandong Province on Datun Coal and Electricity Company' (guanyu shandong sheng zhengshou datun meidian gongsi ziyuanshui wenti de jinji qingshi), Government of Peixian county (GPC), 1 November 1996.

Guo, R. (1993), *Economic Analysis of Border-Regions: Theory and Practice of China* (zhongguo shengji bianjie diqu jingji fazhan yanjiu), Beijing: China Ocean Press.

Guo, R. (1996), *Border-Regional Economics*, Berlin: Springer.

Guo, R. (2009), *How the Chinese Economy Works–Third Edition*, London and New York: Palgrave Macmillan.

Guo, R., S. Li and Y. Xing (2003), 'Ownership Reform and Income Distribution in China's State-Owned Enterprises: The Case Study of Guangzheng and Chuangda' (zhongguo guoyou qiye gaizhi yu zhigong sgouru fenpei: guangzheng gongsi yu chuangda gongsi de anli yanjiu), *Management World*, No. 4, 103–111.

Gustafsson, B. and S. Li (2000), 'Economic Transformation in Urban China and the Gender Earnings Gap'. *Journal of Population Economics*, July, 2000, vol. 13(2), 305–29.

Gustafsson, B. and S. Li (2001), 'The Anatomy of Rising Earnings Inequality in Urban China', *Journal of Comparative Economics*, vol. 29(1), 118–35.

Haggard, S. and S. Webb (1994), 'What Do We Know About the Political Economy of Economic Policy Reform?' *The World Bank Research Observer,* vol. 8(2), pp.143–68.

Hammer, J.S. (1995), 'Public Expenditure and Health Status in China', Policy Research Department, The World Bank, Washington, DC.

Hu, Y. (1992), 'Guizhou Recovers its Broken Roads with the Neighbouring Provinces' (Guizhou yu linsheng xiutong duantou lu), *People's Daily*, 20 September, p. 1.

Huang, Y. (1999), 'State-Owned Enterprise Reform', in R. Garnaut and L. Song (eds.), *China: Twenty Years of Reform*, Canberra: Asia Pacific Press, pp. 95–116.

Hwang, E-G (1993), *The Korean Economies: A Comparison of North and South*, Oxford: Clarendon Press.

Jiang, Z. (1998), 'Speech Commemorating the 20th Anniversary of the Party's Third Plenum of the 11th Party Congress', 19 December, Beijing: the Great Hall of the People.

Jiang, Z. (2002), 'Report to the 16th National Congress of the Communist Party of China', 8 November, Beijing: the Great Hall of the People.

Jin, H., Y. Qian, and B.R. Weingast (2001), 'Regional Decentralization and Fiscal Incentives: Federalism, Chinese Style', mimeo, Stanford University.

Kang, X. (2002), 'An Analysis of Mainland China's Political Stability in the Coming 3–5 Years', *Strategy and Management* (in Chinese), No. 3, 1–15.

Kaufmann, D., A. Kraay, and M. Mastruzzi (2008), 'Governance Matters VII: Aggregate and Individual Governance Indicators, 1996–2007', *World Bank Policy Research Working Paper* No. 4654, Washington, DC: World Bank.

Keidel, A. (1995), 'China's Regional Disparities', Washington, DC: World Bank.

Knight, J. and L. Song (1993), 'Why Urban Wages Differ in China', in K. Griffin and Zhao Renwei (eds) *The Distribution of Income in China*. London: Macmillan.

Lai, D. (1999), 'Education, labour and income distribution' (jiaoyu, laodongli yu shouru fenpei), in Zhao, R., K. Griffin (eds.), *The Household Income Distribution in China* (zhongguo de jumin shouru fenpei), Beijing: China Social Science Press, pp. 451–74.

Lam, W.W. (1999), *The Era of Jiang Zemin*, Singapore: Prentice Hall.

Lau, L., Y. Qian, and G. Roland (2000), 'Reform without Losers: An Interpretation of China's Dual-Track Approach to Reforms', *Journal of Political Economy*, vol. 108, 120–63.

Li, D. (1998), 'Changing Incentives of the Chinese Bureaucracy', *American Economic Review*, vol. 88(2), 393–7.

Li, S. and W. Li (1994), 'Estimating the ratios of return to investment in education in China' (zhongguo jiaoyu touzi de geren shouyilv de guji), in Zhao, R., K. Griffin (eds.), *The Household Income Distribution in China* (zhongguo de jumin shouru fenpei), Beijing: China Social Science Press, pp. 442–56.

Li, W. (1997), 'The Impact of the Chinese Reform on the Performance of Chinese State-Owned Enterprises, 1980–89', *Journal of Political Economy*, vol. 105, 1080–106.

Li, Z. (1993), 'In-Depth Exploration of the Question of Regional Blockades', *Chinese Economic Studies*, vol. 26, no. 5, 23–36.

Liew, L. (1999), 'The Impact of the Asian Financial Crisis on China: the Macro-economy and State-Owned Enterprise Reform', *International Management Review*, vol. 39 (4), 85–104.

Liew, L., L. Bruszt, and L. He (2003), 'Causes, National Costs, and Timing of Reform', Thematic Paper, Washington DC: GDN.

Lin, J. (1992), 'Rural Reforms and Agricultural Growth in China', *American Economic Review*, vol. 82, 34–51.

Lipton, D. and J. Sachs (1990), 'Creating a Market Economy in Eastern Europe: The Case of Poland', *Brookings Papers on Economic Activity*, vol. 75–133.

Litwack, J. and Y. Qian (1998), 'Balanced or Unbalanced Development: Special Economic Zones as Catalysts for Transition', *Journal of Comparative Economics*, vol. 26, 117–41.

Liu, T. (1995), 'Changes to China's Economic System Structure' (zhongguo jingji tizhi jiegou de yanbain), *Management World*, no. 3, 51–6.

Lo, C. (2004), 'Bank Reform: How Much Time Does China Have?' *The China Business Review*, available at: http://www.chinabusinessreview.com/public/0403/chilo.html.

LTB (1995), 'Status Relating to the Cross-Provincial Exploitation of Datun Coal and Electricity Company and Xuzhou Coal Administration' (kuasheng kaicai de datun meidian gongsi, xuzhou kuangwuju youguan qingkuang), the Local Taxation Bureau (LTB), Shandong province, 17 April 1995.

Mastel, G. (1996), 'Beijing at Bay', *Foreign Policy*, vol. 104(Fall), 27–34.

Mastel, G. (1998), 'The WTO and Nonmarket Economies', *The Washington Quarterly*, vol. 21(3), 5–9.

MCA and MWC (1982), 'Report Concerning the Scheme of Re-adjusting the Shandong–Jiangsu Border in Lake Weishan Area' (guanyu sulu liangsheng weishanhu diqu huajie fang'an de baogao), the document of Ministry of Civil Affairs (MCA) and Ministry of Water Conservancy (MWC), (min[1981], No. 68; [1981]shuigui, No. 48, signatures by: Zhang Bangying and Qian Zhengying).

MCI (1997), 'Several Opinions Concerning the Developments of Shareholding and Partnership Enterprises in the Coal Industry', Beijing: Minstry of Coal Industry (MCI), Meibanzi No. 245.

McKinnon, R. (1991a), 'Financial Control in the Transition from Classical Socialism to a Market Economy', *Journal of Economic Perspectives* vol. 5, 107–22.

McMillan, J. and B. Naughton (1992), 'How to Reform a Planned Economy: Lessons from China', *Oxford Review of Economic Policy*, vol. 8, 130–43.

Meadows, D.H., D.I. Meadows and J. Randers (1972), *Limits to Growth: A Report of the Club of Rome's Project on the Predicament of Mankind*, Rome: the Club of Rome.

MOF and MGM (1997), 'Letter Replying to Issues Concerning the Collection of the Mining-Compensated Fees on the Datun Coal and Electricity Company' (guanyu zhengshou daun meidian gongsi kuangchan ziyuan bushangfei de youguan wenti de pifu), Minstry of Finance (MOF) and Ministry of Geology and Minerals (MGM, caijizi [1997], No. 851, 21 November 1997.

MOF and STB (1997), 'Letter on Opinions Concerning the Location of Collection of Taxation on Coal Resources in the Lake Weishan Area' (guanyu weishanhu diqu meitan ziyuanshui nashui didian de yijian de han), Ministry of Finance (MOF) and State Taxation Bureau (STB), caishuizi [1997], No. 55.

Morici, P. (1997), 'Barring Entry? China and the WTO', *Current History*, September, vol. 96, 274–7.

Murphy, K., A. Shielfer, and R. Vishny (1992), 'The Transition to a Market Economy: Pitfalls of Partial Reform', *Quarterly Journal of Economics*, vol. 107, 889–906.

Murrell, P. (1992), 'Evolution in Economics and in the Economic Reform of the Centrally Planned Economies', in C. Clague and G. Raisser (eds.), *The Emergence of Market Economies in Eastern Europe*, Cambridge: Blackwell, pp. 35–53.

NBS (various years), *China Statistical Yearbook*, Beijing: China Statistics Publishing House.

NPC (1979), 'Law of the People's Republic of China on the Joint Ventures with Chinese and Foreign Investment' (zhonghua renmin gongheguo zhongwai hezi qiye fa), Beijing: National People's Congress of China.

NPC (1993), 'Anti-unfair Competition Law' (fan bu zhengdang jingzhen fa), Beijing: National People's Congress of China.

NPC (1997), 'Criminal Law of the People's Republic of China' (zhonghua renmin gongheguo xingfa), Beijing: National People's Congress of China.

OLL (1961), 'Records of the Seventh Meeting of Shandong and Jiangsu Provincial Representatives Concerning the Resolution of Disputes of Peixian and Weishan Counties over the Lakeside Land and Lake-related resources' (shandong jiangsu daibiao guanyu jiejue peixian yu weishanxian hutian, huchan jiufen xietiao huiyi di qici huiyi jilu), 30 October 1961, provided by the Office of Lakeside Land (OLL), Peixian County.

OLL (1984), 'Comrade Wan Li's Speech at the Meeting of Report Delivered by Comrade Cui Naifu of Minister of Civil Affairs on the Issues Concerning the Resolution of the Disputes over Lake Weishan' (wanli tongzhi zai tingqu minzhengbu buzhang cuinaifu tongzhi guanyu jiejue weishanhu zhengyi wenti huibao shi de jianghua), recorded material provided by Office of Lakeside Land (OLL), Peixian county, 1984.

OLL (1996), 'Statistics on Status of the Lakeside Land and Lake-related Resources in Lake Weishan, Peixian County' (peixian guanyu zai weishanhu nei hutian, huchan qingkuang tongji), Office of Lakeside Land (OLL), Peixian county, 8 June 1996.

OLL (1998), 'Status Concerning the Past Resolutions of the Jiangsu and Shandong Provinces over the Four Southern Lakes Disputes' (sulu liangsheng lici xieshang jiejue nansihu zhengyi qingkuang), provided by the Office of Lakeside Land (OLL), Peixian County.

OLL (2000), 'Status Concerning the Implementation of the Three Central Documents' (guanyu guance zhixing zhongyang 'sange wenjian' de qingkuang), Office of Lakeside Land (OLL), Peixian county.

PJWS (1984), 'Summary of the Negotiations Concerning the Fulfillment of the Documents Issued by the CCP's Central Committee (zhongfa[1984], No. 11) and the State Council (guofa[1984], No. 109)' (guanyu guance zhixing zhongfa[1984] 11hao wenjian he guofa[1984] 109hao wenjian de shangtan jiyao), Peixian county, Jiangsu province and Weishan county, Shandong province (PJWS), 8 September 1984.

Portes, R. (1990), 'Introduction to Economic Transformation of Hungary and Poland', *European Economy*, vol. 43, 11–18.

Qian, Y. (2002), 'How Reform Worked in China', draft, also in D. Rodirk (ed.), *In Search of Prosperity: Analytic Narratives on Economic Growth*, Princeton, NJ: Princeton University Press, 2007, pp. 297–333.

Qilu Evening News (1997), 'The Village Surrounded by Polluted Water' (bei wushui baowei de cunzhuang), *Qilu Evening News*, 14 December 1997.

Reti, P. (2001), 'China's Path toward a Market Economy: Interview with a Prominent Reformer', *Transition Newsletter*, Oct.–Nov.–Dec., 17–19.

Richardson, G. P. and A. L. Pugh III (1981), *Introduction to SD Modeling with DYNAMO*, Cambridge, MA: The MIT Press.

Rodrik, D. (1996), 'Understanding Economic Policy Reform', *Journal of Economic Literature* vol. XXXIV (March), 9–41.

Roland, G. (1991), 'Political Economy of Sequencing Tactics in the Transition Period', in L. Csaba (ed.), *Systemic Change and Stabilization in Eastern Europe*, Aldershot: Dartmouth, pp. 47–64.

Sachs, J. (1993), *Poland's Jump to the Market Economy*, Linel Robbins Lectures, London: MIT Press.

Sachs, J. and A. Warner (1995), 'Economic Reform and the Process of Global Integration', *Brookings Papers on Economic Activity*, vol. 1995, No. 1, 1–95.

Sachs, J. and W.T. Woo (1994), 'Structural Factors in the Economic Reforms of China, Eastern Europe, and the Former Soviet Union', *Economic Policy*, vol. 18, No. 1, 102–45.

SBWC (2002), *Weishan Statistical Yearbook 2001*, edited by the Statistical Bureau of Weishan Country (SBWC), May 2002.

SCSR (1996), 'The Environment of Changes in the Role of the Government in China: Analysis of a Survey', in State Commission of System Reform (ed.), *Chinese Economic Almanac 1996*, Beijing: China Statistical Press.

Shen, L. and Y. Dai (1990), 'Chinese Federal Economy: Mechanisms, Impacts, and Sources' (zhongguo de zhuhou jingji: jizhi, houguo he genyuan), *Jingji Yanjiu* (Economic Research Journal), no. 3, 10–3.

Shirk, S. (1993), *The Political Logic of Economic Reform in China*, Berkeley, CA: University of California Press.

State Council (1980), 'Provisional Regulations Relating to the Development and Protection of Socialist Competition' (guanyu fazhan yu baohu shehui zhuyi jingzheng de zhanxing tiaoli), Beijing: State Council.

State Council (1981), 'The State Council's Official Comments on 'Report Concerning the Scheme of Re-adjusting the Shandong-Jiangsu Border in Lake Weishan Area' of Ministry of Civil Affairs and Ministry of Water Conservancy' (guowuyuan dui minzhengbu, shuilibu 'guanyu sulu liangsheng weishanhu diqu huajie fang'an de baogao' de pishi), 1981, State Council, Beijing.

State Council (1982), 'Notice Relating to the Prohibition of Blockades in the Sale of Industrial Products' (guanyu jinzhi gongye chanpin xiaoshou bilei de tongzhi), Beijing.

State Council (1984a), 'Report on Issues Concerning the Resolution of Lake Weishan Disputes' (guanyu jiejue weishanhu zhengyi wenti de baogao), the State Council's Dispatched Working Group to Lake Weishan, Beijing, 9 April 1984.

State Council (1984b), 'The Second Report on Issues Concerning the Resolution of Lake Weishan Disputes' (guanyu jiejue weishanhu zhengyi de dierci baogao), presented by the State Council's dispatched working group, 23 August 1984.

State Council (1986), 'Regulations on Some Issues Concerning the Further Promotion of Horizontal Economic Unification', Beijing: State Council, 26 March.

State Council (1988), 'Regulations of the P. R. China Concerning the Resolutions of the Disputes on Borders of the Administrative Divisions', Beijing: State Council, revised version.

State Council (1990), 'An Administrative Order to Remove all Regional Blockades to Trade', Beijing: State Council.

State Council (1993), 'Temporary Regulations Concerning the Resource Taxation of the People's Republic of China' (zhonghua renmin gongheguo ziyuanshui zhanxing tiaoli), Article 12, Beijing, State Council, No. 139 document, 25 December 1993.

State Council (1994), 'Regulations Concerning the Management of Collection of the Mining-Compensation Fees' (kuangchan ziyuan bushangfei zhengshou guanli tiaoli), Beijing, State Council, No. 150 document, 27 February 1994.

Svejnar, J. (1989), 'A Framework for the Economic Transformation of Czechoslovakia', *Planning Economic Report*, vol. 5, 1–18.

Tang, W. and W. Parish (1998), *The Changing Social Contract: Chinese Urban Life Under Reform,* New York: Cambridge University Press.

Wedeman, A.H. (1993), 'Editor's Introduction to Chinese Economic Studies', *Chinese Economic Studies*, vol. 26, no. 5 (special issue on regional protection), 1–2.

Wei, S. (1993), 'Gradualism vs. Big Bang: Speed and Sustainability of Reforms', Mimeo, Harvard University, Cambridge, MA.

Weishan County Annuals (weishanxian xianzhi), the government of Weishan county, Shandong province, 2000.

Williamson, J. (1995), 'What Washington Means by Policy Reform', *The International Political Economy and the Developing Countries*, vol. 1, 514–28.

WOLA (1998), 'Report on the Work of the Delimitation between Peixian and Weishan Counties' (guanyu peiwei bianjie kanjie gongzuo de huibao), the Working Office of Lake Area (WOLA), Peixian County, 17 February 1998.

Woo, W. (1994), 'The Art of Reforming Centrally Planned Economies: Comparing China, Poland and Russia', *Journal of Comparative Economics*, vol. 21, 276–308.

World Bank (1996), *From Plan to Market: World Bank Development Report 1996,* New York: Oxford University Press.

Wu, J. (2005), *Understanding and Interpreting Chinese Economic Reform*, Mason, OH: Thomson South-Western.

Wu, R.-I (1996), 'Importance of Integrating China and Taiwan into the WTO System', *Journal of Northeast Asian Studies*, vol. 15, No. 3.

Wu, J. and R. Zhao (1987), 'The Dual Pricing System in China's Industry', *Journal of Comparative Economics*, vol. 14(Nov.), vol. 11(3), 309–18.

Xu, D. (1995), 'China: Contradictory Measures Frustrate Bank Reform', *Economic Reform Today* (Banking and Financial Reform), No. 1, Center for

International Private Enterprise, Washington, http://www.cipe.org/ publications/fs/ert/e15/china.htm.

Young, A. (2000), 'The Razor's Edge: Distortions and Incremental Reform in the People's Republic of China', *Quarterly Journal of Economics*, vol. 115(4), 1091–136.

Yu, J. (2004), 'Why We Don't Believe Economists', *Sohu Online Paper* (in Chinese), 15 September, available at: http://culture.news.sohu.com/ 20040915/n222055879.shtml.

Zhao, R. (1998), 'Professor Gu Zhun's Academic Career and Emotional Experience', draft, CASS, Beijing.

Zhao, R. (1999), 'Review of Economic Reform in China: Features, Experiences and Challenges', in R. Garnaut and L. Song (eds.), *China: Twenty Years of Reform*, Canberra: Asia Pacific Press, pp. 185–200.

Zhao, Y. (2001), 'Earnings Differentials between State and Non-State Enterprises in Urban China, Working paper series No. E2001001, Peking University, Beijing, China.

Zhuravskaya, E. V. (2000), 'Incentives to Provide Local Public Goods: Fiscal Federalism, Russian Style', *Journal of Public Economics*, *76*(3), pp. 337–68.

Zichuan Annuals (1990), compiled by the Office of Annuals of the government of Zichuan district, Shandong province.

INDEX

behavior, 31, 32, 33, 52
behavioral problems, 52
behaviours, xi, 17
Beijing, xvi, 25, 40, 45, 49, 71, 73, 74, 77, 87,
    89, 97, 99, 100, 112, 113, 114, 115, 116,
    117, 119, 120, 121
beliefs, 53, 71
benefits, 27, 30, 38, 55, 89
Big Bang, 120
birth, 46, 80
bonds, 54
bonus, 61, 62, 63, 65, 67
bonuses, 62, 65
borderline, 76, 84, 92
Boston, xvi
BSR, xi, 28, 29, 30, 31, 32, 33, 109
Buenos Aires, xvi
bureaucracy, 25, 45, 46

C

campaigns, 2
cancer, 80
capitalist, 26, 55
CAS, 73
cement, 59
central bank, 37, 53, 105
Central Europe, 111, 113
central planning, 2, 55
CEO, 109
channels, 36
children, 24, 46
Civil War, 36
class struggle, 1
classes, 27
closed economy, 6
Co, 104, 105
coal, 58, 59, 64, 70, 74, 88, 93, 96, 97
coal mine, 70
Cold War, 36
collaboration, xv
colleges, 65
collusion, 21, 22, 26, 27, 55
commerce, 49, 93
commercial bank, 53

commodities, 2, 44, 50, 53, 95
commodity, 2, 50, 95
communication, 71, 80, 92, 100
communism, 55
Communist Party, 1, 23, 75, 77, 83, 99, 109,
    112, 115
communities, 88
comparative advantage, 36, 65
compensation, 49, 51
competition, 26, 40, 54, 95
complex systems, 8
complexity, 9
compliance, 27
components, 4, 57
composition, xiii, 25, 63
concealment, 40
concrete, 28
confidentiality, 23
conflict, 79, 84, 86, 87, 92, 94
conflict resolution, 84
confrontation, 33
confusion, 92
Congress, 4, 23, 25, 48, 103, 109, 110, 115,
    117
consensus, 27
Constitution, 105
construction, 4, 77, 80, 86, 92, 96
consumer goods, 49
consumers, 49, 63
control, 1, 4, 7, 38, 40, 45, 50, 52, 53, 77, 86,
    101
convergence, 57
corporate governance, 54
correlations, 6, 8
corruption, 3, 27, 38, 40, 47
costs, 22, 24, 30, 43
covering, 76
CPI, 63
credentials, 100
credibility, 40, 56
credit, 54
crops, 77
cross-border, 72, 73, 79, 84, 88, 92, 93, 94,
    96, 97, 101
crown, 46

poor, 26, 27, 38
population, 9, 44, 52, 71, 76, 80, 82, 101, 102
positive feedback, 8
poverty, 27, 57
power, 3, 22, 26, 28, 31, 37, 40, 45, 96
power plant, 96
preference, xiii, 30
pressure, 25, 40
prevention, 74
price index, 63
prices, 47, 51
private, 4, 25, 48, 100
private enterprises, 25
private ownership, 48
private sector, 4
privatization, 106
product market, 50
production, 2, 43, 44, 49, 58, 59, 64, 65, 74, 80, 82, 86, 89, 95, 101, 105
production quota, 44
productivity, 69
profit, 61
profitability, 24
profits, 58, 61
program, 4, 23, 27, 38, 43, 54, 56, 84
property, vi, 26, 48
property owner, 26
prosperity, 2, 57, 93
protection, 72, 80, 97, 120
public, 2, 4, 6, 38, 40, 75, 80, 86, 88, 92, 95, 97, 100, 101, 105, 116
public finance, 4, 95

R

radio, 47
rain, 77
range, 26
reading, 23
real terms, 44
reality, 25
reception, 100
recessions, 58
recognition, 77
reconstruction, 59

redistribution, 22, 24, 88, 93, 96
reforms, xi, 3, 4, 5, 11, 22, 24, 25, 27, 28, 29, 31, 33, 34, 35, 36, 37, 41, 43, 44, 45, 46, 47, 48, 52, 53, 54, 55, 56, 58, 59, 62, 64, 65, 95
refractory, 59
regional, 3, 52, 53, 57, 71, 88, 105, 120
regression, 67, 69
regressions, 67, 68, 69, 70
regulated economy, 6, 8, 9, 10, 12, 18
regulation, 2, 49
regulations, 25, 49, 72, 73, 93, 97
relationship, 21, 51, 52
relationships, 58
religious belief, 53, 71
religious beliefs, 53, 71
renminbi, 110
rent, 37
Republican, 38
Republican Party, 38
reserves, 77
reservoir, 74
resistance, 35, 48, 74
resolution, xiii, 72, 73, 77, 82, 83, 84, 89, 93, 94, 98, 99, 100
resource management, 88
resources, 43, 54, 59, 65, 72, 74, 80, 81, 82, 83, 87, 88, 89, 93, 96, 97, 99, 100, 101, 117
respiratory, 110
responsibilities, 1, 38
retaliation, 26
retardation, 41
retention, 51
retirement, 23, 46
retirement age, 46
retrenchment, 5
revenue, 51, 53, 64, 95
rice, 95
rigidity, 5
risk, 31, 37, 54
risk management, 54
rivers, 71, 72, 74, 80, 92
Roads, 114
Rome, 116
Rubber, 59

Y